THE PAINTINGS
OF
HANS HOLBEIN THE YOUNGER
COMPLETE EDITION
BY PAUL GANZ

—

PHAIDON

SAINT URSUS. DETAIL FROM PLATE 47

THE PAINTINGS OF HANS HOLBEIN

FIRST COMPLETE EDITION
BY PAUL GANZ

PHAIDON PUBLISHERS INC

DISTRIBUTED BY OXFORD UNIVERSITY PRESS · NEW YORK

MADE IN GREAT BRITAIN
INTRODUCTION AND CATALOGUE PRINTED BY ROBERT MACLEHOSE AND CO. LTD. GLASGOW
TWO COLOUR PLATES PRINTED BY HENRY STONE AND SON LTD. BANBURY
FOUR COLOUR PLATES AND MONOCHROME PLATES PRINTED BY EMIL BIRKHÄUSER ET CIE. A. G. BASLE

CONTENTS

PREFACE

THE aim of the present volume is to give a comprehensive survey of the whole of Hans Holbein the Younger's pictorial œuvre, by means of reproductions and in the form of a catalogue containing the most important data on each individual work.

In order to give a clearer idea of the scope of Holbein's achievement in various fields, the reproductions have been divided into four groups, each group being arranged chronologically and supplemented by illustrations of details. The series of plates begins with the religious works, then come the portraits, the miniatures, and the decorative works. Reproductions of works which are in a bad state of preservation, further details, and supplementary illustrations serving for purposes of comparison and identification, will be found in the catalogue. In the portrait section, replicas of lost portraits of King Henry VIII have been added as pendants to those of his wives of which the originals have been preserved; among the miniatures, certain items of doubtful authenticity have been included, as they are all very closely related to the master's work and in any case serve to supplement it. The murals have been reproduced as fully as possible by showing not only the few fragments still extant, but also copies of lost works, Holbein's own sketches for the originals and copies of these. Our reproduction of the 'Holbein Table-top' in Zurich conveys for the first time the impression which the painting made originally; this was achieved by retouching the negatives and covering up the portions that were rubbed off in the course of time.

I have not included in the catalogue lost works known to us only through engravings or late copies. Where these are mentioned, the reference is to Volume XX of *Klassiker der Kunst*, published in 1912.

As regards the state of preservation of works by Holbein cleaned and restored during the last few decades, it should be noted that, when the old varnish was removed, their highest lights and parts of the pigment came away with it and had to be replaced by the restorers.

Except in the case of two works from his early period, I see no reason to correct my previous attribution to Holbein of certain recently discovered works, and I must also continue to affirm my rejection of certain attributions made by other scholars, e.g. 'The Judgement of Solomon' (Öffentliche Kunstsammlung, Basle, Inventory No. 153), the 'Portrait of Prebendary Zimmermann' (Germanisches Museum, Nuremberg), the 'Portrait of a Young Man' (in a private collection in New York), which was published in *Phoebus*, 1949, Vol. II/2, and the small round picture of a 'Bearded Man' (Uffizi, Florence).

I also stand by the dates which I have hitherto assigned to the various works, though I have mentioned the opinions of other scholars when these differ from my own, in order to show the difficulty of dating works of art and to facilitate future research into this problem. In my opinion it is wrong to base one's chronological arrangement on stylistic features alone if these are contradicted by the evidence of one's senses and by the few documents available.

I have been at pains to show, by reproducing numerous details, some of them in the size of the original, as many as possible of the beautifully painted accessories, as these give an insight into the greatness of Holbein's talent. For the same reason, all the colour plates are devoted to the reproduction of such details.

I am indebted to my son, Dr. Paul Leonhard Ganz, for his valuable collaboration in the preparation of the catalogue, and to Mr. Ludwig Goldscheider for his assistance in procuring the excellent photographic material, which has made it possible to show for the first time all the pictures in their entirety.

My thanks, and those of the publishers, are also due to the owners of works by Holbein for permission to reproduce them. His Majesty the King has graciously given permission to include the pictures from the Royal Collection. Further acknowledgements are due to His Grace the Archbishop of Canterbury, the Duke of Buccleuch, the Marquess of Cholmondeley, the Earl of Radnor, Lord Methuen, and George Howard, Esq.; to the directors of the National Gallery and the Victoria and Albert Museum in London, of the National Gallery of Art in Washington, of the Metropolitan Museum in New York, and of the museums of Boston, Philadelphia and Saint Louis; also to Duveen Bros. Inc., New York, for photographs and information. I also have to thank the directorate of the Schweizerische Landesmuseum in Zurich, the Gesellschaft für schweizerische Kunstgeschichte, and the Keepers of the Museums in Basle and Solothurn for their kind collaboration.

Lastly I must express my warmest thanks to Dr. B. Horovitz, the director of Phaidon Press Ltd., who has spared neither pains nor expense in the production of this book.

OBERHOFEN AM THUNERSEE, 1949   PAUL GANZ

HANS HOLBEIN THE YOUNGER

THREE COUNTRIES—Germany, Switzerland and England—claim the right to consider Hans Holbein the Younger as their own, and this fact alone gives him an international status. He was born in Germany and, as the son of a painter, received a sound training there. In the Swiss city of Basle he was able to develop his gifts in the most varied fields of the formative arts; it was in Basle that he matriculated as a 'master' and, as a citizen of the city republic, perfected his art. And finally in England, to which he first paid a short visit when the political upheaval in Basle led to a shortage of commissions from his patrons, and to which he afterwards returned for good, he rose to the zenith of his artistic achievement and fame.

Hans Holbein is called 'the Younger' to distinguish him from his father Hans, a leading master of the Late Gothic school in Augsburg. The son was born during the winter of 1497–98, as can be deduced from the ages given on a drawing of him by his father and on the last of his own self-portraits. He left home in 1514, travelling by way of Constance to Basle, where he and his elder brother Ambrosius apprenticed themselves to Hans Herbster, a painter of note in that city. Even at this early age Hans Holbein soon made a name for himself as an illustrator among the printers of Basle. His work then took him to Lucerne, whence he crossed the Gotthard to Northern Italy. On his return to Basle, he matriculated in the guild 'zum Himmel' and set up as an independent painter. After the death of his brother, he married the widow of a master tanner who had been killed at the battle of Marignano. From now on his activities embraced every branch of the formative arts. In addition to numerous altar-pieces, he executed the mural paintings in the Basle town hall, decorations on the façades of houses, portraits and many designs for glass painting. But the bulk of his work consisted of designs for woodcuts, among these being the celebrated series of the 'Dance of Death' and the 'Illustrations to the Old Testament'. In the spring of 1524 he made a journey to France, visiting Lyons and Avignon, where he was able to study French Renaissance art on the spot and enlarge his technical knowledge. In the autumn of 1526 he gave up his workshop in Basle and went to the Netherlands, presumably travelling down the Rhine valley. In Antwerp he visited Quentin Matsys and then he went to England, where, with the help of Sir Thomas More and other friends, to whom he had been recommended by Erasmus of Rotterdam, he earned his living as a portrait-painter, achieving success both from the artistic and from the economic point of view.

After two years in England, he returned to Basle. Here he was able to purchase two houses and was commissioned by the new masters of the city to complete the frescoes in the city hall by painting the third wall of the Council Chamber, which had remained empty. But this and other commissions for Basle publishers, for Erasmus and for a small circle of friends, did not satisfy him, and even the Council's offer of a pension for his family could not induce him to remain in Basle. He decided to settle permanently in London, where portrait-painting would always assure him a remunerative living.

The first portraits which he painted after his return to London are dated 1532, the sitters being country gentlemen from Norfolk and German merchants from the Steelyard in London. In 1528 Holbein had painted the portraits of John Godsalve of Norwich and his father, and it may have been Godsalve who introduced him to the merchants of the Steelyard, for in 1532 Godsalve entered

HANS HOLBEIN THE YOUNGER AND HIS BROTHER AMBROSIUS. Painting by Hans Holbein the Elder

the service of Thomas Cromwell and, as controller of customs duties on foreign silks, was in contact with the Hanseatic merchants. Two portraits of Godsalve and one of his wife testify to the closeness of their relationship and Godsalve may well have introduced Holbein to the county families, to the Hanseatic merchants and to his master Thomas Cromwell, whom Holbein painted for the first time in 1534, when Cromwell was still Keeper of the King's Treasure. As Cromwell shortly afterwards became secretary to King Henry VIII, his influence being thereby greatly increased, Holbein's entry into the service of the court may well have been due to him, especially as his first commission was to paint the hall of the Privy Council, to which Cromwell belonged.

As one of the official court painters, Holbein was assigned a workshop of his own in the tower of Whitehall Palace, which a hundred years later was still known as 'Holbein's Gate'. The King made use of him for all kinds of work. In addition to portraits of members of the royal family and the extensive wall and ceiling paintings, since lost, in the royal palaces, Holbein had to design the King's state robes, from the buttons set with jewels down to the buckles on his shoes, and also the robes, golden necklaces and pieces of jewellery which Henry presented to his various wives. He also had to make designs for table silver, ceremonial weapons, seals, book-bindings and all the other articles in daily use at the court. Such was the King's confidence in Holbein that he attached him to the delegations which proceeded abroad to inspect prospective brides, thereby ensuring that he would receive portraits of the ladies which were absolutely true to life. Holbein became the leading portrait-painter of England and it is estimated that during his second stay there he painted nearly one hundred and fifty portraits, large and small. In addition, he devoted himself to the applied arts, especially to goldsmith's work, and over 250 designs, most of which are now preserved in the British Museum and in Basle, bear witness to his flair for making the best use of his materials and for endowing every single article with the highest degree of artistic beauty. In October 1543, Holbein fell a victim to the plague which at that time was raging in London.

THE BROTHERS AMBROSIUS AND HANS HOLBEIN THE YOUNGER. Silverpoint drawing by Hans Holbein
the Elder. Berlin, Print Room

Holbein's biography is a dry recital of facts, revealing almost nothing of his personality, his character, his family life or his relations with his fellow-men in general. Although he twice left his family behind, the first time for two years and the second time for twelve, we possess no letters or other writings of his which would enable us to form an estimate of his character. Nor is there any reference to this in Erasmus of Rotterdam's voluminous correspondence or in the literary remains of Bonifacius Amerbach. We know only that he apprenticed both his sons to goldsmiths, that the younger, Jakob, came to England after his father's death and died there in 1552, and that the elder, Philipp, first worked in Lisbon and then settled at Augsburg. In Holbein's will, which he made on 8th October 1543 in the presence of four witnesses, his family in Basle is not even mentioned, but from another document, dated 29th November of the same year, we learn that Hans of Antwerp was appointed executor and that Holbein had died in the meantime in the parish of St. Andrew Undershaft.

Even the portraits by his father's hand and the three self-portraits contribute little to our knowledge of the man, for the latter have been much distorted by subsequent retouchings. Nevertheless the portrait his father painted of him as a youth and the drawing in which he appears as a boy of fourteen, show two characteristic features—a penetrating, keenly observant glance and an unfriendly, sulky expression, lacking both in cordiality and in trust in his fellow-men. The Basle self-portrait shows him as an independent master, with the red painter's cap perched on his broad, bony skull; the second self-portrait, painted in 1538 during a visit to Basle, shows him as painter to the King's court, while the third, dating from 1542-43, exists only in the form of a sketch (Florence) and a round picture (Indianapolis) and several miniature replicas. Glance and expression have changed little with the passing of the years, from which we may conclude that Holbein's character and attitude towards his fellow-men had also undergone little change. His consistently good relations with Henry VIII, whose favour he contrived to keep until his death, throw an interesting sidelight on his character.

The art of Hans Holbein the Younger is founded upon his unusual talent and his cool apprehension of the outward appearance of things, undisturbed by sentiment or personal feeling. His vision is so penetrating that in depicting what he sees, he manages to reproduce not only the characteristic features of any object, but also, when dealing with human beings, the invisible characteristics of their inmost being. The relationship between an artist and nature is the key to the proper understanding of his art, and the manner in which he reproduces and gives life to the world around him is a measure of the spiritual force through which he exercises his creative gifts. Holbein strove to achieve the utmost degree of truth to nature and a faithful reproduction of the material world around him. His vision penetrated the subject and extracted its essentials; discarding everything immaterial, he discovered new beauties, hitherto unsuspected, in nature and reproduced her inexhaustible variety without resorting to sensuous charm or exaggerated effects. He approached every model, even the human model, with objective impartiality, and by emphasizing the essentials, gave his rendering of it a subjective style. Holbein's draughtsmanship was simple; line was the means by which he rendered form, indicated movement and suggested expression. It remained the sure foundation even of his painting, and gave to his figure compositions, his portraits and even his decorative works an astonishing clarity and an organically coherent solidity. Holbein's father, who was his teacher, was a gifted draughtsman with a keen eye for the beauties of nature, and the son was able to learn from his father how an altar-piece may be built up from carefully chosen impressions of the surrounding world and from the varied episodes of everyday life. But Holbein's vision was keener than his father's; he detected the peculiarities of his subject with the thoroughness of a scientific investigator, without allowing himself to be drawn into deeper problems by the promptings of sentiment or fantasy. He had a three-dimensional grasp of every object as a definite circumscribed body in space and placed it, as a part of the whole, in its correct place in the picture, where it fulfilled the function he had assigned to it. He was less interested in the episode than in the true and convincing reproduction of the action; he depicted biblical episodes with the same objectivity as he did ordinary episodes of human life, without any trace of Christian piety or mysticism. His story of the Passion consists of a series of historical scenes—the corpse of Christ in the tomb and his pictures of the Dance of Death are ruthless reminders of human frailty, in which he himself takes no personal interest. This same clear realism gives to all his biblical scenes a version of the episode which can be understood by all and enabled him, in the midst of the violent struggles which followed the beginning of the schism within the Church, to produce propaganda pictures for and against the Papacy, without ever assuming a definite position of his own. Every one of his works is based on unswerving and ruthless observation of reality, uninfluenced by external events. This is true of his portraiture as well—he sees only reality, the external phenomenon, and, with that subjective concentration which is peculiar to him, he conceives it as an integral whole comprising all that is to be seen.

His innate feeling for form was so strong, that, in the course of his artistic development, he was able to absorb every external influence, using the trends of foreign art and the works of foreign artists which influenced him merely to widen and strengthen his own style, which matured in its own natural way. Direct imitations, such as his Last Supper after Leonardo's fresco in Milan, can rarely be identified among his works, but on the other hand we frequently find compositional borrowings from contemporary works of art, especially in his early works and in his religious compositions.

If the Dutch art historian, Carel van Mander, in his book on painting published in 1618, speaks of the 'excellent Holbein', praises his versatility and claims that 'in oil, water-colour, miniature and everything he has equal mastery', this must not be taken as denoting unqualified recognition of his technical ability. As a draughtsman he had learned from his father the use of silverpoint, and he also made use of pen and wash, the chiaroscuro process of the Italians and the three-crayon method of the French; similarly, as a painter, he adopted the technical devices of the Lombard school—the enamel-like lustre of colouring, the exquisitely delicate modelling, the metal-like polish of crayon groundwork and the use of resin as a binding vehicle, and he improved his methods by studying French and Flemish painting. In the last portraits painted during his first stay in England his brilliant colouring is already simplified by the introduction of a monochrome blue background, which he subsequently softened to harmonize with the tints of his sitters' countenances, a very effective means of rendering expression which was often used by French artists, but is seldom so delicately differentiated as it is in Holbein's portraits. Probably influenced by Titian's portraits, which he may well have seen in Brussels or Paris, he heightened the effect of his portraits by a further simplification, achieving monumental effect by reducing the colouring to a threefold harmony of flesh, draperies and background.

Despite a certain tendency to virtuosity in his painting technique, its basis was always the drawing. His sketched design, the preliminary study, was transferred to the ground with pen and grey wash, being often modelled like a wash drawing, with sharply defined lines drawn in later, for which geometrical instruments, such as compasses and set-square, were used. Holbein painted in dry colours, with a fluid binding vehicle probably composed of resin and linseed. Local colour he applied smoothly in pure tints, rendered more lustrous by a thin layer of transparent colour. For the blue background he used a mineral colour made from azurite and malachite, sometimes on a black foundation, but always so thickly applied as to be higher than the other colours. The deep glaze and the enamel-like lustre of the colouring were achieved by means of the metallic, highly polished crayon groundwork, which admitted of few corrections and, like the preliminary sketch, remained visible through the thin layer of colour.

In draughtsmanship and painting, Holbein's art has the same two outstanding qualities—the symmetry of composition peculiar to his work and the technical perfection of the execution.

The first works which can be assigned to the young Holbein are religious pictures, at that time the chief product of his father's workshop in Augsburg, which turned out numerous altar-pieces, ex-votos and other devotional works. Their style is that of the last phase of Late Gothic, in which Flemish influences can be discerned behind the stark realism, and the personages, including the saints, were portrayed from living models. The art of the younger Holbein had its origin in his father's workshop, as can be seen from his use of motives from the works of his father and other Augsburg masters, from the crudely realistic representation and the joy in narration, for instance in the 'Bearing of the Cross' (1515), in the marginal drawings for the 'Praise of Folly' and the pictures on the table-top made for the Basle 'banneret' Hans Baer. The mural paintings in the interior of the Hertenstein house at Lucerne, begun in 1517, represented similar scenes in the same narrative style—episodes from the owner's life, showing him with his wife and son riding out to hunt deer and ducks, a tournament, a battle and two humorous scenes, a fountain of youth, the removal of the beggars from the castle—in the same manner as the rape of women, the sleeping shopkeeper and the Nobody on Baer's table. The scenes from classical history on the façade of the house, which in accordance with the humanistic tendency of the time were used to symbolize human virtues and vices, were nothing new for Holbein, as he had executed similar subjects for title-page blocks in Basle. The lower half of the façade, however, contains new decorative motives —imaginary buildings, antique statues, an abundance of Early Renaissance ornaments and two friezes of putti—all pointing to a study of Italian Renaissance art in Lombardy. A few years later, when he painted the 'House of the Dance' in Basle, Holbein attempted to combine the various motives into an integral composition, by transforming the two house walls into a four-storey Renaissance building seen from two sides. The motives used on the Hertenstein house were further developed and to them he added whole triumphal arches, rows of columns and archways with coffered ceilings, without, however, abandoning the genre-like accessories. The decorative intention is of greater importance than the organic construction, which is no more convincing than the architectural features of his designs for painting on glass, executed in the first part of his second stay in Basle. That Holbein studied and eventually solved this problem is proved by the somewhat later design for the façade of the '*Haus zum Kaiserstuhl*'.

It was probably thanks to these two series of mural paintings and the recommendation of his patron Jakob Meyer zum Hasen, that Holbein was entrusted with the execution of mural paintings in the newly-erected hall of the Grand Council in Basle, for which the humanist Beatus Rhenanus chose the subjects and wrote the relevant inscriptions. Holbein surmounted the difficulties of the unfavourable location by using imaginary architecture such as he had seen in Italy, and gave the room the appearance of an open portico by dividing up the walls by means of pilasters, columns and statues in niches, and treating the intervening spaces as apertures through which open-air scenes from ancient history could be discerned. The work was begun in summer 1521, but was interrupted in November 1522, by which time the paintings on the west side-wall and the long wall—five historical pictures and eight allegorical statues—had been completed. The narrative is not vivid, but it is didactic, which was in accordance with the spirit of the commission and may have had some connection with the gruesome nature of the episodes. On the other hand, the perspective treatment of the buildings and of the statues in their niches is more effective and more logical than on the two house façades. The design for the façade of the '*Haus zum Kaiserstuhl*' suggests that Holbein may have executed other mural paintings at this time, but this, though probable, cannot be established with certainty. During the following years, before his departure for England, he developed his decorative style still further towards that monumental simplicity and plastic power of expression to be seen on the painted wings of the door of the organ-casing in Basle Cathedral, on which in 1526 he painted four mighty figures, two reliefs and a lifelike reproduction of Renaissance oakwood carving.

Although Holbein went to England with the intention of earning his living as a portrait-painter, it is possible that he also had the opportunity of executing wall paintings there, Chamberlain believes that he can be identified with a 'Master Hans', who from 15th January to 4th April 1527 was employed, at a salary of four shillings per diem, on the decoration of a banqueting hall erected at Greenwich for the reception of King Francis I of France, and who executed a large painting on canvas for the adornment of the triumphal arch. It is true that Holbein painted the portraits of Sir Henry Guildford, under whose supervision the banqueting hall was erected, and of Sir Bryan Tuke, who effected the payments, but that fact alone is not sufficient to prove that the identification is correct. On the other hand, it is quite possible that he executed the painting of Sir Thomas More and his family, for which he made a sketch soon after his arrival, as a mural painting for a room in their new house at Chelsea and that subsequent occupants of the house destroyed it. French sculpture, with which he became acquainted during his journey to France in the spring of 1524, must have enlarged his spiritual horizon, and his association with Sir Thomas More and his circle must also have furthered his artistic development. The two paintings of Rehoboam and the Meeting between Saul and Samuel, with which he adorned the third wall of the Council Hall in Basle in the summer of 1530, differ from all his earlier works in their greater simplicity of composition, the keynote of the episodes being more strongly accentuated. In depicting the cortège of the returning army he found the solution to the problem, which he had already attacked in the 'Bearing of the Cross', of depicting an advancing multitude, a problem to which he returned once again two years later in the mural paintings for the hall of the Hanseatic merchants in London, where he achieved classical beauty in his rendering of the Triumphs of Riches and Poverty, after the pattern of Italian 'Trionfi'.

The monumental paintings which Holbein executed for Henry VIII have vanished, but various eye-witnesses have left us descriptions of extensive series of pictures. The only authenticated picture is that painted for the Privy Chamber in the Palace of Whitehall, in which the Privy Council held its meetings. It showed the King and his third wife, Jane Seymour, together with the King's parents, all in life-size, standing on either side of a commemorative tablet in front of a richly ornamented Renaissance building, on which could be seen the initials of the royal couple, joined in a lovers' knot, and the date 1537. The left half of the preliminary sketch and a copy of the whole picture have been preserved and give us a good idea of the original, which was destroyed by fire in 1698. The figures in their ceremonial attitude were so lifelike that visitors entering the room often believed they were entering the presence of the King himself. According to Pepys, the ceiling of the Matted Gallery may also have been painted by Holbein. His last great mural painting, showing Henry VIII confirming the privileges of the Barber Surgeons, who are kneeling before the King on his throne, was designed and begun by Holbein, but was not completed until after his death. Among Holbein's later works, we also possess designs for a number of wall paintings, but we do not know for what buildings they were destined or whether they were ever executed. At all events they were all intended for the King, e.g. the 'Visit of the Queen of Sheba to Solomon', painted on vellum in grisaille, blue and gold. This work, full of figures and carefully executed down to the last detail, could achieve its monumental effect only as a mural picture of large dimensions; it may be considered Holbein's greatest achievement in this field and the crowning example of his monumental style. The architectural background is similar to that of the Whitehall painting, but the spatial effect is infinitely more grandiose and heightens the solemnity and the classical beauty of the scene. The conversation between Solomon, to whom Holbein has given the features of Henry VIII, and the Queen of Sheba is counterbalanced by the dignitaries standing on either side of the throne and the approaching procession of beautiful women, and by the devotion of the servants offering the gifts. Every single figure is a masterpiece in itself, yet contributing to the artistic effect of the whole. The disappearance of all the master's mural paintings is an irreparable loss, for the sketches and designs which have been preserved cannot compensate for the lost originals.

No complete altar-piece by Holbein has come down to us in its original form, but from his extant religious pictures and from the numerous Old and New Testament episodes which he drew as designs for paintings on glass or for woodcuts, we can trace the same stylistic develop-

ment as we have just seen in his historical pictures. After his stay in Milan the dramatic movement of his early 'Passion' series is replaced by a more tranquil and subdued rendering of the
subject, which, like the works of Italian artists, invites the spectator to pious contemplation.

Holbein uses the high, narrow pictorial field preferred by Lombard artists for their pictures of
saints; this format enabled them to achieve greater spatial depth, and the pictures were combined,
side by side or in superimposed rows, to form altar-pieces enclosed in richly carved, gilded
Renaissance frames. The polyptych by Bernardino Butinone and Bernardo Zenale, which the
two artists painted in the last decade of the fifteenth century for the collegiate church of San
Martino in Treviglio, is an outstanding example of the decorative diversity and fine, coherent
effect of such altar-pieces.

It is possible that the first work which Holbein executed after his return from Italy, the
religious picture for the convent of the Barefoot Friars in Lucerne, was not an altar-piece with
wing-panels, but a series of pictures combined in a frame after the Italian manner. Shortly
afterwards Holbein created his 'Passion' in eight episodes, arranged in two rows and separated
by painted and gilded borders, and we can well imagine that if these were to be enclosed in a
richly carved Renaissance frame, they might form an independent altar-piece, which would
provide a more logical explanation for the unilateral painting than the generally accepted theory
that they were intended as wing-panels for the 'Last Supper'.

From Italian religious paintings Holbein took not only the decorative effect, but also their
style and the plastic mode of representation, the proportions of the human figure, the system of
juxtaposition, the delicately executed mimicry of the figures, the antique draperies, the architectural motives and the carefully balanced symmetry of the composition. Italian ornamentation
was already known to him through the engravings of Nicoletto da Modena and Zoan Andrea.

Holbein never contrived to give to the figure of the Saviour an interpretation of his own and
instead of giving the features an expression of suffering, he reproduced them without a trace of
feeling, or else, as in his renderings of the 'Crucified Christ', concealed them in the shadow of the
bent head. On the other hand, he attempted to raise the realistic narrative above the earthly
plane by means of supernatural sources of light. In the Nativity of the wing-panel for the
Freiburg altar-piece, the light emanating from the newborn Child fills the whole room, while in
its pendant, the Adoration of the Magi, the rainbow-coloured star of the Wise Men hovers
amidst bright clouds above the ceremonial scene. A halo-like brilliance surrounds the head of the
Solothurn Madonna and in the '*Noli me tangere*' the radiance of the two angels illuminates the
empty tomb. In the nocturnal scenes and in the darkness of Golgotha of the eight episodes from
the 'Passion', he also creates a strange and anxious atmosphere, like the morning light in which
Christ appears to Mary Magdalen. Such motives Holbein could find in the works of his contempo-
raries to the north of the Alps, for instance in Dürer, who since the days of his Apocalypse
woodcuts had studied the problems of supernatural lighting, in Matthias Grünewald and in Hans
Baldung Grien, whose chief works Holbein must have seen in Isenheim and Freiburg before 1520.

This group of religious works created after the artist's return from Italy was produced within
a few years. It gives us an idea of the impressions which Holbein brought back from Como and
Milan, and shows how he could absorb foreign conceptions of art without abandoning his own
style. His first works of this kind, the Lamentation at the foot of the Cross in Lucerne, the two
chiaroscuro paintings of the 'Man of Sorrow' and the 'Mater dolorosa', the 'Last Supper' after
Leonardo and the 'Passion' in eight scenes, are still strongly influenced, in their composition and

colouring, by the art of Leonardo and the Lombard school. But in the wings for the Freiburg altar-piece we find Holbein already combining Italian forms with Northern conceptions, and in the ten drawings for the 'Passion' and in his illustrations for the Old Testament he achieves his own style, which he carries to a monumental conclusion in his decoration for the organ-wings and in the still later altar-piece of the Madonna which he painted for the Burgomaster Jakob Meyer.

Nevertheless, Holbein owes his world-wide fame, not to these pictures, but to his portraits. As early as 1516, in the second year of his stay in Basle, he produced the first characteristic example of these—the double portrait of Jakob Meyer zum Hasen and his wife. It may well be that a portrait by the Augsburg artist Burgkmair, similar in construction, served him as a model, but what is of more importance is the precision of the preliminary drawing and the harmonious juxtaposition of the two sitters, so completely different in stature and character. The sharp delineation of the expression is not so noticeable in the painted version as it is in the preliminary silverpoint sketches, for Holbein did not learn the beauty of colour effect and the secret of freer and natural pose of the figures until after he had studied the works of Leonardo's pupils, for example Solario's portrait of the Chancellor Morone and the numerous profile portraits by Ambrogio de Predis and Bernardino dei Conti. The profile portrait of the young Basle scholar Bonifacius Amerbach, painted in October 1519, shortly after Holbein's return from Italy, reflects the impressions he had received in that country. The noble conception of the sitter, the natural poise of the body, the clever insertion of the young humanist's own poem on a tablet, without prejudice to the dominating poise of the expressive head, and the depth of spatial effect, all mark the beginning of a new phase in Holbein's development. To precision of draughtsmanship is now added the invigorating effect of unbroken colours. This fascinating portrait of Amerbach must have induced many art-lovers in Basle to have themselves portrayed by Holbein, even if that had not already been the fashion, but few examples of such portraits have remained—some small half-lengths, a few profile heads and the nine portraits of members of the Oberried-Tschekkenbürlin family on the wings of the Freiburg altar-piece, executed in 1521–22.

It is probable that the portrait of Holbein's patron, the printer and publisher Johannes Froben (Hampton Court), also dates from this time, for it was at Froben's instigation that Holbein painted the portraits of Erasmus of Rotterdam, who lived in Froben's house in Basle from 1521 on. A first profile portrait, preserved in the form of a woodcut dated 1522, may have been intended as a pendant to the portrait of Froben, a humanistic notion giving pictorial form to the collaboration between author and publisher, which Quentin Matsys had already made use of in his double portrait of Erasmus and Petrus Aegidius, painted in 1517–18 for Sir Thomas More. With these works Holbein entered the international field, for of the four portraits painted in the years 1522–24, two went to England and one to France, as Erasmus tells us in a letter to Pirckheimer in Augsburg dated 3rd June 1524. At this time Holbein was able to see and study the 55-year-old, ailing scholar in the surroundings of his home in Basle and to reproduce his frail external appearance, his noble spiritual expression and his uncommon powers of concentration with such vividness that our modern conception of Erasmus the Sage is still based on Holbein's portrayal of him. He portrayed Erasmus in profile and with head three-quarters turned; the profile version, sharply defined and at the same time delicately conceived, gives the aged countenance a monumental grandeur and emphasizes the spiritual personality more strongly than the genre-like version of the scholar in his study. Nevertheless, the latter painting, dated 1523, is a valuable contribution from the human standpoint, for it gives us the atmosphere, the tranquillity of the room in which the great scholar studied and wrote his books, always standing upright as a result of his bodily constitution. Holbein's execution has improved still further since the portrait of Amerbach—the skin and the individual features, e.g. the eyes, are characterized with scientific skill down to the smallest detail, with the result that the general impression is strengthened, while the colouring softens the sharpness of the drawing. How conscientiously Holbein took his work is shown by two sketches (now in the Louvre) which were preliminary studies for the outlines of the face and the hands of the Longford Castle portrait; they reveal his astounding powers of observation and show how he strove to achieve the highest degree of lifelikeness even in painting. The still-life by the curtain, the soft lustre of the fur, every hair of which can be seen, the shrivelled skin of the wrinkled hands, are all masterly achievements, but all this sinks into insignificance beside the expression of Erasmus, plunged in thought and staring straight in front of him, with its mingling of spiritual maturity and philosophical calm. Though the spatial problem has not quite been solved, uniformity is achieved by heightening the colouring to a degree of solemn majesty; the colour is in harmony with the dignified gravity of the sitter and emphasizes it.

Study of French portraiture during his journey to Lyons and Avignon gave Holbein a fresh opportunity of developing his own conceptions. The clear thinking of the French, their logical simplification of the prevailing style of portraiture, which emphasized the strong personalities of men and the gentle charm of women, were in accord with his own cool conception. We do not know for certain whether he came into direct contact with the artists then working in Lyons, the foremost of whom, according to Madeleine Huillet-Istria, was Jean Perréal, but he got to know the 'trois crayons' technique and, in fact, used it himself on his journey home, when he sketched the portrait statues of the Duke and Duchess of Berry in the Lady Chapel of Bourges Cathedral. These sketches show the artist's interest in French figure sculpture, but the huge figures executed as monumental portraits on the wings of the organ casing in Basle reveal its influence on his own works. The two allegorical portraits, in which he depicted Magdalena Offenburg, a high-born, but somewhat frivolous young lady of Basle, as Venus and Lais of Corinth, also show French influence in their subject-matter and in the delicate treatment.

Among the best portraits which Holbein created before his journey to England are the three studies for the portraits of the Meyer family in the painting of the Madonna now in Darmstadt. These preliminary sketches in coloured chalk are more pictorial in conception than the studies for earlier works, and the general impression is livelier and more natural. The lines are still very sharply drawn, but are more mobile and more delicate in conception than when executed with the metal pencil, while the surfaces between the contours achieve the spatial value necessary for the pictorial effect thanks to the generous use of coloured chalk. Thus equipped, Holbein could measure his strength against the English, Italian and Dutch artists then working in London.

The 1523 portrait of Erasmus, formerly in the possession of Archbishop Warham of Canterbury at Lambeth Palace, was the starting-point of Holbein's activity during his first stay in London. This prince of the Church had himself portrayed in the same attitude, standing before a curtain behind his prie-dieu, with the addition of the insignia of his high office, the mitre and crozier. Holbein retained the three-quarter turning of the head and added to the picture, even when he was not executing formal portraits, objects relating to the activity of the sitter. Thus he showed the astronomer Kratzer at his work-table, surrounded by measuring instruments, the man of letters Godsalve writing a letter, a young lady from the animal-loving circle of Sir Thomas More

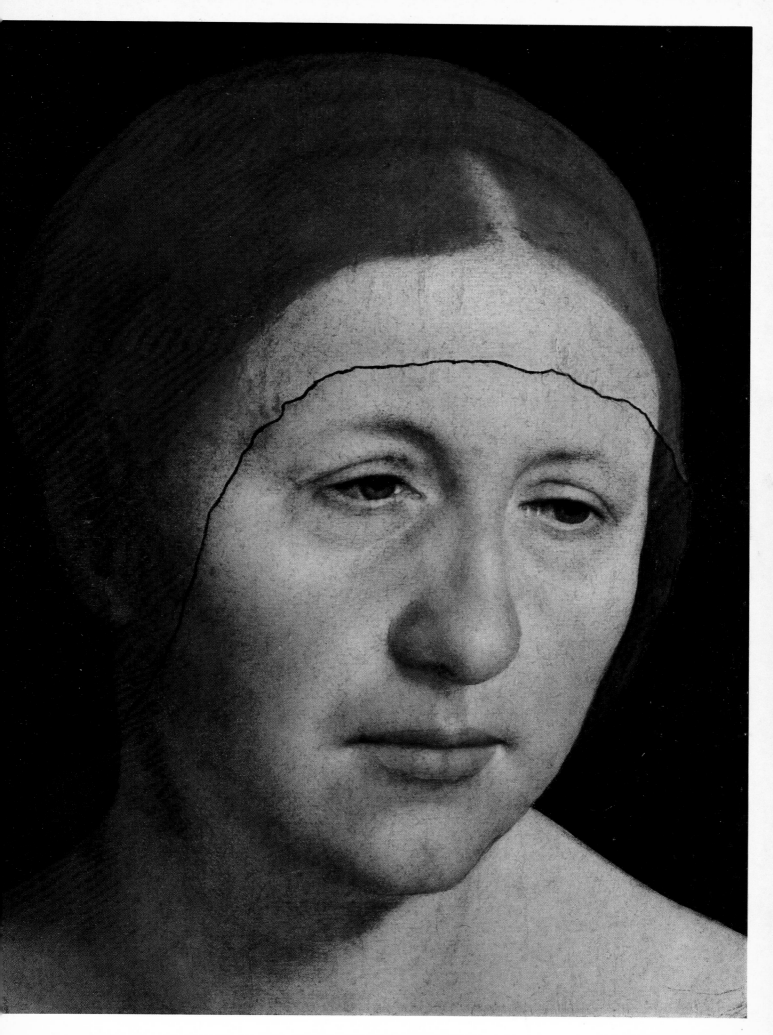

HOLBEIN'S WIFE. DETAIL FROM PLATE 89

with a squirrel and a magpie. As the practical-minded English seem to have attached some value to the indication of the sitter's name and age, e.g. on the bench in the portrait of Sir Thomas More and on the pillar in that of Lady Guildford, Holbein sometimes resorted to riddles and painted in the background of the portrait a slip of paper, covered with writing and closed with sealing-wax. Later, when he introduced the blue background, he found a better solution in the use of decorative Latin capital letters as part of the linear composition, these appearing for the first time in the indication of name and age and the motto in the portrait of Sir Bryan Tuke. That Holbein's psychological intuition was deepened and refined by his intercourse with his highly cultured clientele, is only natural, and it is certain that he derived the greatest benefit in this respect through Sir Thomas More, with whose family he lived for a time. With the aid of Sir Thomas, he created the life-size group, showing all those members of the family who were living together in the Chelsea house, grouped around the head of the family and conversing on literary problems. The idea and the arrangement of the personages according to rank and age may have been due to Sir Thomas, but this does not detract from Holbein's achievement, for with this work he created the first family group to be produced north of the Alps, in which the participants are shown, not assembled in religious worship, but in a well-furnished room adorned with flowers, engaged in tranquil conversation. The preliminary sketches for the individual portraits were executed by Holbein in the same crayon technique that he used for the above-mentioned studies in Basle, but the design is more grandiose and the feeling more delicate. Even in the sketch for the whole picture, giving only the outlines, every individual is so admirably characterized that Erasmus, on receiving it, wrote to Sir Thomas that it would be impossible for him to see the family more clearly even if he were there.

The masterpiece of Holbein's portraiture, the group of his own family which he had left behind in Basle, was painted after his return from England, but not later than 1529. It shows his wife, once beautiful, but prematurely aged by care and sorrow, and his two children, staring joylessly into space, the figures being lifesize and arranged in the form of an isosceles triangle, whereby the intimacy of the relationship between mother and children is heightened. With merciless realism Holbein depicts the pitiable aspect of his nearest and dearest, without, however, betraying his own feelings as a man. His art of portrayal is so great that he grasps the slightest reflection of spiritual emotion and achieves the miracle of revealing his wife's inmost thoughts through her eyes, troubled by sickness and clouded with weeping. In classical form, the external and inner portrait of a human being is here fused into an integral whole, which makes this picture one of the greatest achievements of the art of portraiture. Of equal lifelikeness is the small round portrait of Erasmus, also dating from this period, which surpasses all the other portrayals of the scholar made at that time for his numerous admirers.

During his second stay in England, which brought him his greatest successes as a portrait-painter, Holbein's art was not further enriched. The demand for his works compelled him to abridge his processes. His preliminary studies were reduced to a minimum of details, but they were sufficient to enable him to paint his portraits, which he contrived to build up from memory with infallible accuracy. In individual cases, such as the 'Ambassadors' and the first portraits of Henry VIII and Jane Seymour, he doubtless made more thorough preliminary studies, but these must have been matters of more careful observation and not, as in the case of the 1527 portrait of Sir Thomas More and the group of his own family, based on execution in the presence of the sitters. High personages had neither the desire nor the time to grant the artist long sittings.

B

In this last period of his work Holbein's portraits comprise every format, from lifesize full-lengths to bust portraits in miniature size. Bust portraits or half-lengths including hands, in three-quarters life-size, were sufficient for most of his sitters, and Holbein usually represented the heads three-quarters turned against a monochrome blue background. If, to heighten the characterization, he reproduced the whole milieu in which the sitter lived, for example the counting-house of the Hanseatic merchant Georg Gisze or the office of the King's Treasurer, Thomas Cromwell, such detailed interiors served merely as a framework for the figure portrayed. Often a curtain or a few green twigs in the background sufficed to indicate the location, as in the portraits of Sire de Morette and Derich Born. Holbein depicted his models standing behind a stone parapet or a table covered with objects, holding in their hands articles indicating their professions and social standing. Thus, merchants are seen holding letters bearing their names and addresses, officials hold scrolls and the highest dignitaries their insignia of office. Many also carry gloves to emphasize their social rank. The ladies are depicted either standing or seated, usually in tranquil, passive attitudes with folded hands. In the last self-portrait Holbein depicted himself holding brush and pot of colours.

Three-quarter lengths and full-lengths were reserved for the most eminent personages. Of formal pictures of this kind two or more replicas often exist, e.g. the portraits of the Archbishop of Canterbury and of Thomas Cromwell as Lord Chancellor, and the various portraits of Henry VIII.

The existence of replicas is a consequence of the custom whereby persons of high rank like the King and his Ministers, or artists and scholars such as Erasmus of Rotterdam, often presented portraits of themselves to others. Henry VIII used to present portraits of himself to all his new foundations, to hospitals and universities which he patronized, and some of these institutions are still in possession of these portraits. He also gave portraits of himself to the families of his various wives, e.g. to the Seymours and the Howards, or to his favourites, as can be proved by documents. The only criterion as to the authenticity of such replicas is the artistic quality, for Holbein's originals were often copied exactly and with the aid of his own technique. The same is true of the replicas in smaller format, the little round pictures painted on wooden caskets, and the miniatures measuring not more than two or three inches, which were usually set by jewellers in costly frames and worn as pendants. That Holbein himself also produced masterpieces of miniature-painting, with which he surpassed his teacher Lucas Horebout, the son of a Ghent miniaturist, is proved by a number of extant works dating from after the middle thirties. Horebout was also one of Henry's court painters, and like most other painters in London at that time, was later influenced by Holbein.

That all these replicas are derived from Holbein's originals, even if they only represent a portion, e.g. the bust of a half-length, is supported by the fact that in the replicas made by the artist himself, e.g. those of his portraits of Erasmus, he concentrated on the heads.

During the last ten years of his life, Holbein created nothing new in the way of portraiture; the works of this period reveal a uniform, sharply defined style, conciseness of composition in the outlines, in the treatment of light and in the sitter's expression, thereby achieving an immediate effect which remains. It is impossible to forget Holbein's portraits. If we want to know how he achieved this effect, the answer lies in his calm faithfulness to life, undisturbed by any touch of sentiment, in his preliminary sketches reduced to the essential indications of form, the modelling in full light without the disturbing influence of shadows and the harmony of a few colours, which give the highest degree of animation to the drawn portrait. By systematically confining himself to the simplification of his sitter's outward appearance, as required by the formula of his style, Holbein produced masterpieces of portraiture. His art is honest and true; it never exaggerates and it flatters no one, but endeavours to do justice to all within the limits of an unbiased realism, guided by a keen intellect oblivious to the promptings of the heart.

In his advice to artists Leonardo da Vinci wrote that 'the mirror is our teacher', and against the background of his time this makes the art of Holbein comprehensible, for his realism was based on a thorough knowledge of men and of the world around him, so that his renderings are strikingly lifelike. Herman Grimm, the first scholar to study Holbein, detected nearly a hundred years ago the fundamental trait of Holbein's character, his striving after absolute faithfulness to nature, and said of him: 'No painter has equalled him in characterization. How natural, in him, are coldness and cool realism! He is not a poet, but a historian, for whom the lives of men contain no fairy-tales and no secrets.'

Holbein was one of the first to profit by the intellectual and artistic achievements of artists from other lands and he created a style of his own which knows no local or international frontiers. Wherever he went, he studied the products of the formative arts and thereby enriched his own talent. South German thoroughness and sober outlook on life were his starting-points, but while he was still an apprentice in Basle, he absorbed new influences from the West and from the South, and also became acquainted with the temperamental genre-pictures of the Swiss illustrators Urs Graf and Niklaus Manuel, the graphic art of Dürer and the paintings of Hans Baldung, some of whose motives he used in his own compositions. His stay in Lombardy developed his ideas of Renaissance art to such a degree that it transformed his style. He studied the works of Bramante and of Italian sculptors in Milan, Pavia and Como, and also the technique of Leonardo's pupils, but the decisive experience was the knowledge he gained of the art of Leonardo himself, whose influence appears again and again throughout his career. In France, figure sculpture revealed to him new beauties of charm and quiet grandeur, and with the aid of French portraiture his style achieved monumental proportions. On his way to London he saw works of art in Frankfurt and Cologne, and through Quentin Matsys became acquainted with Flemish art. As a result of the broadening of his artistic knowledge, his composition bore fruit and his technical ability increased, but his own individuality as an artist was not impaired. He was guided by his native talent and this enabled him to exploit these outside influences.

Even today, and despite the fact that his monumental paintings have been lost, the art of Holbein offers us an abundance of unusually beautiful works which exemplify his artistic aims, so that he has every right to be counted among the greatest masters of all times and of all schools. His art is a synthesis of strict realism and a feeling for the beauty of form and the harmony of proportions. It endows every one of his works with an inner tension and an external equilibrium, which combine to produce the highest degree of artistic effect. His supremacy does not lie in the wealth of his invention or in a sharply-defined temperament, but in the faithful reproduction of everything visible and in the cleverness which enabled him to accomplish every task in the manner most suited to its purpose.

IOANNES HOLPENIVS BA... SILEENSIS

SVI IPSIVS EFFIGIATOR   Æ: XLV.

SELF-PORTRAIT OF HANS HOLBEIN. Florence, Uffizi (Cat. No. 131)

THE PLATES

RELIGIOUS PAINTINGS

QVE·VIRG·PEPERIT·VIRG·Q·PERMANET·LACTAVIT·PROPRIIS·VBERIBVS·CIEV
PORTANTEMQ·GEREBAT·VLNIS·PRONA·TREMENTIBVS·M·D·XIIII·

1. (Cat. No. 1) THE HOLY VIRGIN ENTHRONED IN GLORY, ADORED BY ANGELS. 1514
Basle, Öffentliche Kunstsammlung

2. (Cat. No. 2) VIRGIN AND CHILD UNDER A RENAISSANCE PORCH. 1515. London, Art Dealer

7. (Cat. No. 5) THE AGONY IN THE GARDEN. 1515/17. Basle, Öffentliche Kunstsammlung

8. THE BAND OF SOLDIERS WITH LANTERNS AND TORCHES, LED BY JUDAS. Detail from Plate 7

9. (Cat. No. 6) THE SCOURGING OF CHRIST. 1515/17. Basle, Öffentliche Kunstsammlung

10–11. (Cat. No. 7–8) HEADS OF TWO SAINTS. About 1515. Basle, Öffentliche Kunstsammlung

12. (Cat. No. 9) ADAM TEMPTED BY EVE. 1517. Basle, Öffentliche Kunstsammlung

13. (Cat. No. 11) THE MAN OF SORROWS. 1519/20. Basle, Öffentliche Kunstsammlung

14. (Cat. No. 12) MATER DOLOROSA. 1519/20. Basle, Öffentliche Kunstsammlung

15. (Cat. No. 13) THE LAST SUPPER, AFTER LEONARDO DA VINCI. About 1520. Basle, Öffentliche Kunstsammlung

16. (Cat. No. 14) THE TWO SHUTTERS OF AN ALTAR-PIECE: THE PASSION OF CHRIST. About 1520. Basle, Öffentliche Kunstsammlung

17–18. THE AGONY IN THE GARDEN; THE KISS OF JUDAS
Left upper part of Plate 16

19–20. CHRIST BEFORE CAIPHAS; THE SCOURGING OF CHRIST
Right upper part of Plate 16

25. JUDAS LEADING THE SOLDIERS. Detail from Plate 17

26. THE PRAYER IN THE GARDEN. Detail from Plate 17

27. ST. PETER STRIKING MALCHUS. Detail from Plate 18

28. ARCHITECTURE IN TORCH LIGHT. Detail from Plate 19

29. PHARISEES, SOLDIERS AND THE HOLY VIRGIN AT THE FOOT OF THE CROSS. Detail from Plate 23

30. CHRIST ON THE CROSS. Detail from Plate 23

31. (Cat. No. 15) CHRIST IN THE TOMB. 1521. Basle, Öffentliche Kunstsammlung

32. HEAD OF THE DEAD CHRIST. Detail from Plate 31

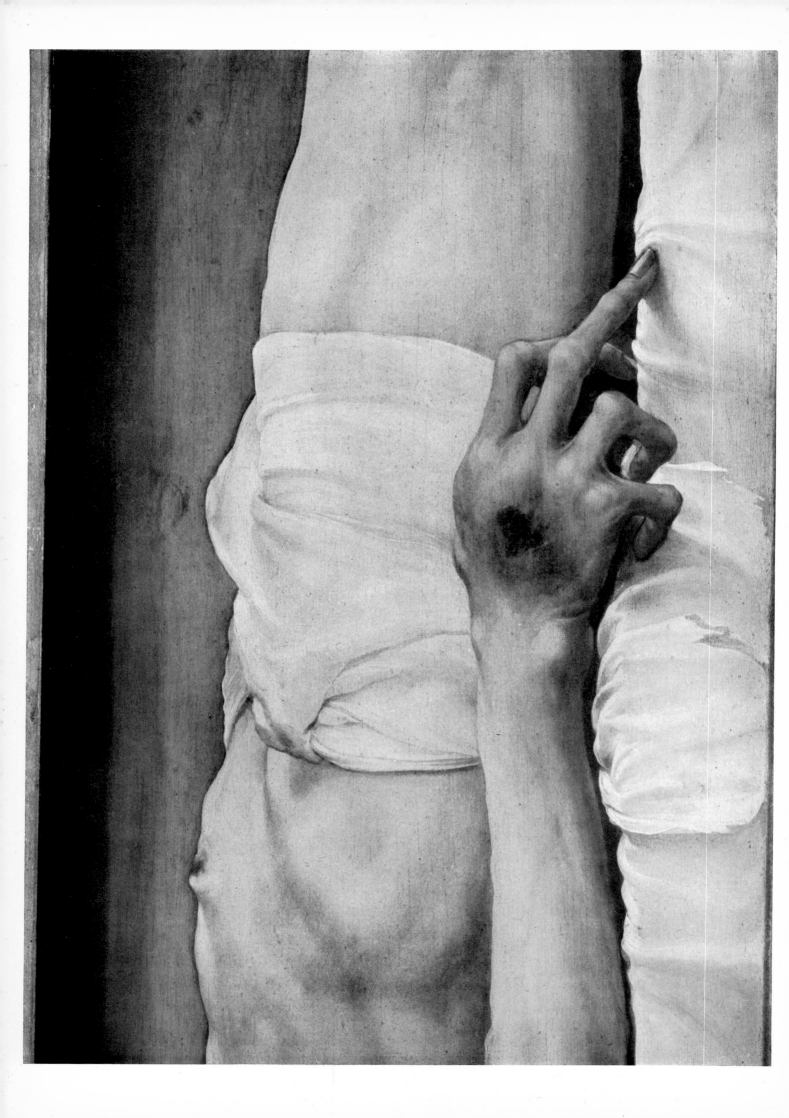

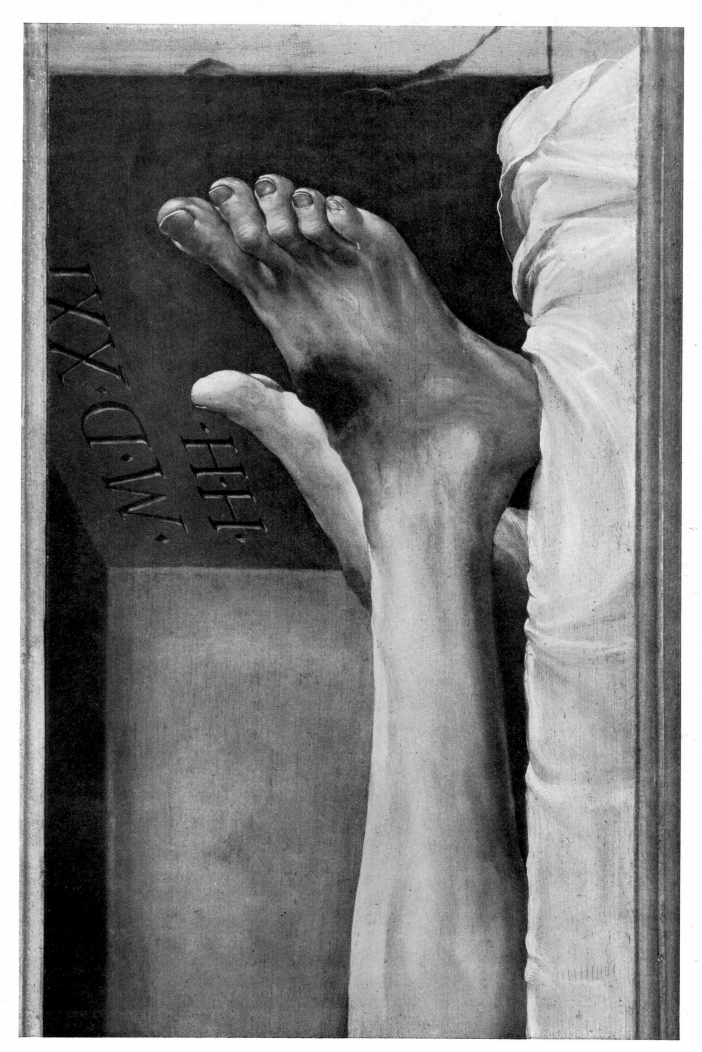

34.

33–34. THE DEAD CHRIST. Details from Plate 31

35. (Cat. No. 16)
NATIVITY AND ADORATION OF
THE SHEPHERDS. 1520/21. Inner
side of the left shutter of the Oberried altar-piece. Freiburg im Breisgau, Cathedral, University Chapel

36. (Cat. No. 17)
ADORATION OF THE KINGS.
1520/21. Inner side of the right
shutter of the Oberried altar-piece.
Freiburg im Breisgau, Cathedral,
University Chapel

37. HANS OBERRIED, TOWN COUNCILLOR OF BASLE, AND HIS TWO ELDEST SONS. Detail from Plate 35

38. AMALIE TSCHEKKENBÜRLIN, THE DECEASED WIFE OF HANS OBERRIED. Detail from Plate 36

39. THE SHEPHERD BEHIND THE COLUMN. Detail from Plate 35

40. ANTIQUE STATUE OF A GODDESS AND ROMAN PILLAR HEADS. Detail from Plate 35

41. RIDERS IN THE RETINUE OF THE THREE HOLY KINGS. Detail from Plate 36

42. THE ADORATION OF THE CHILD. Detail from Plate 35

43. THE STAR OF BETHLEHEM SHINING OVER RUINED BUILDINGS. Detail from Plate 36

44. KING BALTHAZAR IN FRONT OF AN IVIED NICHE. Detail from Plate 36

45–46. (Cat. No. 19–20) ST. GEORGE AND ST. URSULA. 1522. Karlsruhe, Staatliche Kunsthalle

47. (Cat. No. 21) THE ALTAR-PIECE OF JOHANN GERSTER, TOWN CLERK OF BASLE: THE SO-CALLED SOLOTHURN MADONNA. 1522
Solothurn, Kunstmuseum

48. ST. NICHOLAS AND THE BEGGAR. Detail from Plate 47

49. HEAD OF ST. MARY: A PORTRAIT OF HOLBEIN'S WIFE. Detail from Plate 47

51.   MARY MAGDALEN WITH THE ALABASTER BOX OF OINTMENT.   Detail from Plate 50

50.   On opposite page. (Cat. No. 22) NOLI ME TANGERE: CHRIST APPEARING TO MARY MAGDALEN. Hampton Court, H. M. The King

Reproduced by gracious permission of His Majesty The King

51.

52–53. CLOUDED SKY AT DAWN; THE TWO ANGELS SITTING IN THE SEPULCHRE. Details from Plate 50

54. ST. JOHN AND ST. PETER. Detail from Plate 50

56.

56. VIRGIN AND CHILD. Detail from Plate 55

55. On opposite page. (Cat. No. 23) ALTAR-PIECE WITH THE MADONNA OF MERCY AND THE MAYOR MEYER FAMILY,
THE SO-CALLED DARMSTADT MADONNA. 1528/29. Darmstadt, Grandducal Palace

57. THE TWO SONS OF THE MAYOR JACOB MEYER. Detail from Plate 55

PORTRAITS

58. (Cat. No. 24) YOUNG MAN WITH A RED BERET. 1515. Darmstadt, Hessisches Landesmuseum

59. (Cat. No. 25) JACOB MEYER, MAYOR OF BASLE (Pendant to Plate 60). 1516. Basle, Öffentliche Kunstsammlung

60. (Cat. No. 26) DOROTHEA KANNENGIESSER, THE SECOND WIFE OF JACOB MEYER (Pendant to Plate 59)
1516. Basle, Öffentliche Kunstsammlung

61. (Cat. No. 27) BENEDIKT VON HERTENSTEIN, TOWN COUNCILLOR OF LUCERNE. 1517. New York, Metropolitan Museum

62. (Cat. No. 30) BONIFACIUS AMERBACH, PROFESSOR AND JURISPRUDENT OF BASLE. 1519
Basle, Öffentliche Kunstsammlung

63. HANS OBERRIED, AN ALDERMAN OF BASLE. Detail from Plate 35

64. (Cat. No. 34) ERASMUS OF ROTTERDAM, STANDING BEHIND A TABLE. 1523. Longford Castle, Salisbury, Earl of Radnor

65. (Cat. No. 35) ERASMUS OF ROTTERDAM, STANDING AT HIS DESK AND WRITING. 1523. Basle, Öffentliche Kunstsammlung

66. (Cat. No. 36) ERASMUS OF ROTTERDAM, STANDING AT HIS DESK AND WRITING. 1523/24. Paris, Musée du Louvre

67. (Cat. No. 37) SELF-PORTRAIT OF THE ARTIST. 1523/24. Basle, Öffentliche Kunstsammlung

68. (Cat. No. 38) A YOUNG WOMAN, PROBABLY THE ARTIST'S WIFE. 1523/24. The Hague, Mauritshuis

69. (Cat. No. 39) MAGDALENA OFFENBURG AS VENUS. About 1526. Basle, Öffentliche Kunstsammlung

:LAIS: CORINTHIACA: 1526

70. (Cat. No. 40) MAGDALENA OFFENBURG AS LAÏS CORINTHIACA. 1526. Basle, Öffentliche Kunstsammlung

71. (Cat. No. 41) SIR THOMAS MORE. 1527. New York, Frick Collection

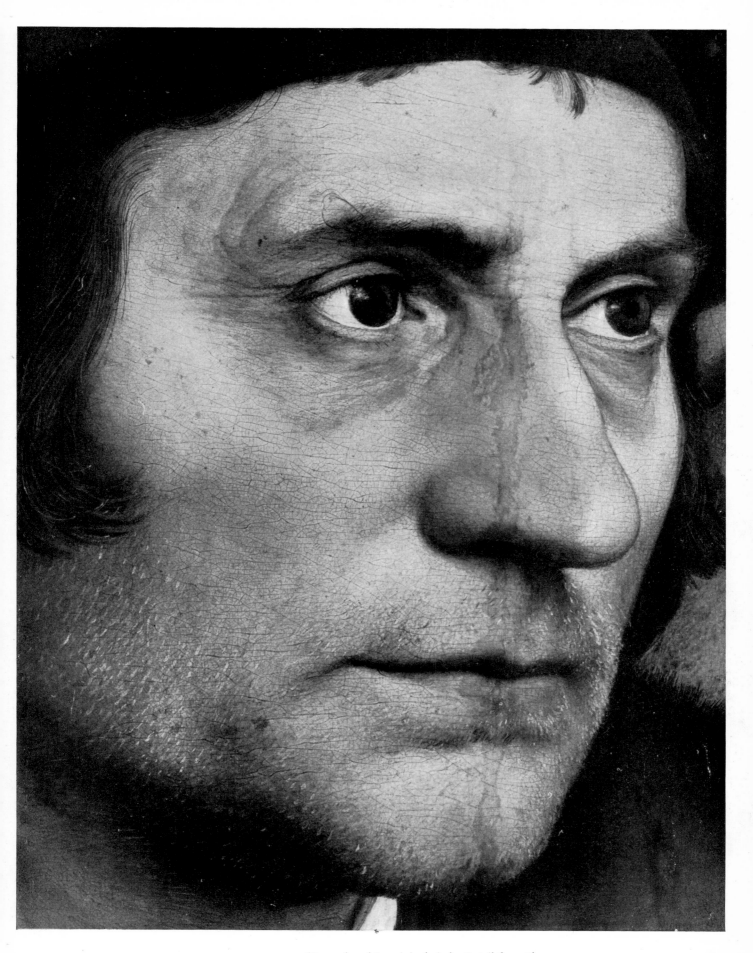

72. SIR THOMAS MORE (Reproduced in original size). Detail from Plate 71

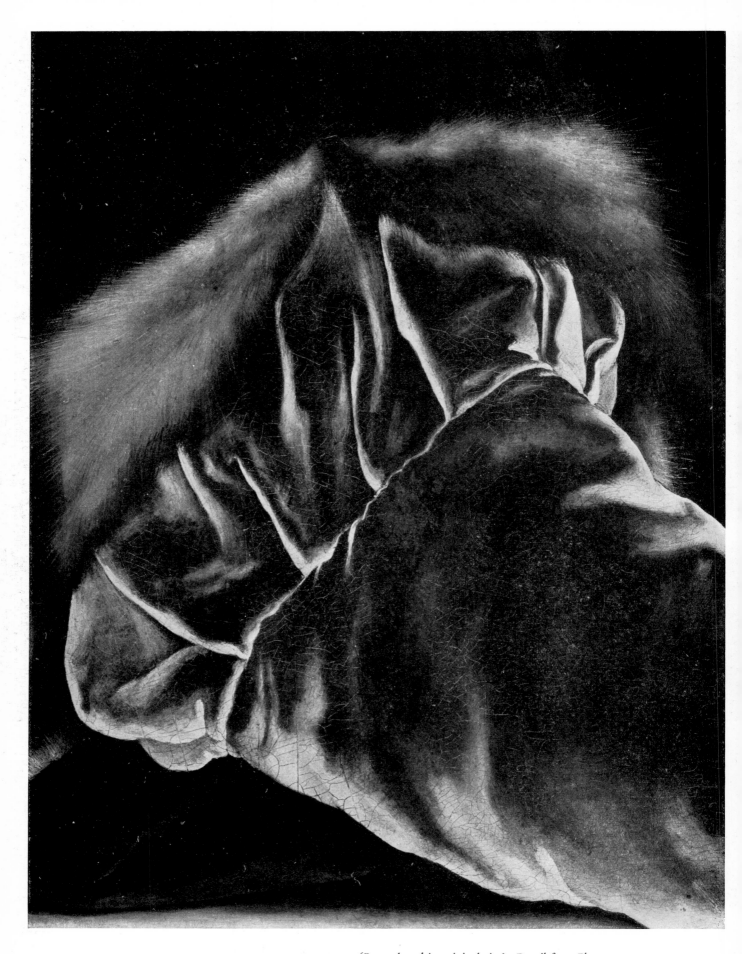

73. VELVET SLEEVE WITH FUR TRIMMING (Reproduced in original size). Detail from Plate 71

74. COLLAR OF SS WITH PORTCULLIS CLASP AND TUDOR ROSE (Reproduced in original size). Detail from Plate 71

75. (Cat. No. 43) LADY WITH SQUIRREL AND MAGPIE. 1527/28. Houghton Hall, Norfolk, Marquess of Cholmondeley

76. (Cat. No. 42) LADY ALICE MORE. 1527. Corsham Court, Lord Paul Methuen

77. (Cat. No. 44) SIR HENRY GUILDFORD, CONTROLLER OF THE ROYAL HOUSEHOLD (Pendant to Plate 78). 1527. Windsor Castle

Reproduced by gracious permission of His Majesty The King

78. (Cat. No. 45) LADY MARY GUILDFORD (Pendant to Plate 77). 1527. St. Louis, U.S.A., Fine Art Museum

79. DOUBLET OF PATTERNED CLOTH OF GOLD, AND THE COLLAR OF THE ORDER OF THE GARTER WITH THE PENDANT GEORGE. Detail from Plate 77

80. HEAD OF LADY GUILDFORD. Detail from Plate 78

81. (Cat. No. 46) WILLIAM WARHAM, ARCHBISHOP OF CANTERBURY (first version). 1527. London, Lambeth Palace

82. (Cat. No. 47) WILLIAM WARHAM, ARCHBISHOP OF CANTERBURY (second version). 1527. Paris, Musée du Louvre

83. EPISCOPAL CRUCIFIX OF GOLD AND JEWELS, WITH WARHAM'S COAT-OF-ARMS AND HIS MOTTO
(Reproduced in original size). Detail from Plate 82

84. PRAYER BOOKS AND THE ARCHBISHOP'S JEWELLED MITRE
(Reproduced in original size). Detail from Plate 82

85. (Cat. No. 48) NIKLAUS KRATZER, ASTRONOMER TO KING HENRY VIII. 1528. Paris, Musée du Louvre

Anno Dñi · M·D·XXVIII

86. (Cat. No. 49) THOMAS GODSALVE AND HIS SON JOHN. 1528. Dresden, Staatliche Gemäldegalerie

87. (Cat. No. 50) SIR HENRY WYATT. 1527/28. Paris, Musée du Louvre

88. (Cat. No. 51) SIR BRYAN TUKE. 1528/33. Washington, National Gallery of Art (Mellon Collection)

89. (Cat. No. 52) THE ARTIST'S WIFE AND HIS TWO CHILDREN. 1528–29. Basle, Öffentliche Kunstsammlung

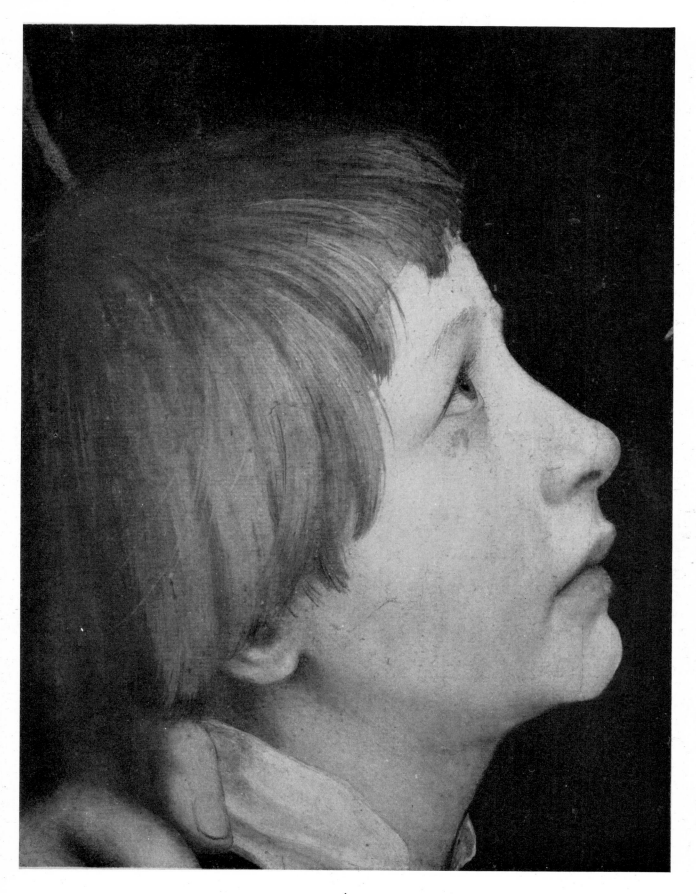

90. HEAD OF PHILIPP, THE ARTIST'S ELDER SON. Detail from Plate 89

91. (Cat. No. 23) ANNA, JACOB MEYER'S DAUGHTER, WITH HER BRIDAL CROWN. Detail from Plate 55

92. (Cat. No. 23) MAGDALENA BAER, THE DECEASED WIFE OF JACOB MEYER, AND DOROTHEA KANNENGIESSER, HIS SECOND WIFE
Detail from Plate 55

93. (Cat. No. 23) JACOB MEYER, MAYOR OF BASLE. Detail from Plate 55

94–95. (Cat. No. 53) PORTRAIT OF PHILIPP MELANCHTHON;
AND DECORATION ON THE INSIDE OF THE COVER
1529–30. Hannover, Landesmuseum

96. (Cat. No. 54) JOHANNES FROBEN, THE GREAT BASLE PRINTER. 1531/32
Maidenhead Thicket, Sir Thomas Merton

97. (Cat. No. 60) ERASMUS OF ROTTERDAM AS AN OLD MAN. 1531/32. Basle, Öffentliche Kunstsammlung
(Enlarged reproduction)

98. (Cat. No. 61) THE HANSEATIC MERCHANT GEORGE GISZE OF DANZIG. 1532. Berlin, Deutsches Museum
99. On opposite page. PINK CARNATIONS IN A GLASS VASE. Detail from Plate 98

100. (Cat. No. 62) A HANSEATIC MERCHANT, THE SO-CALLED GOLDSMITH HANS OF ANTWERP. 1532. Windsor Castle

Reproduced by gracious permission of His Majesty The King

102. (Cat. No. 64) A HANSEATIC MERCHANT, THE SO-CALLED GOLDSMITH HANS OF ANTWERP. After 1533
Schloß Blankenburg, Herzog Ernst-August zu Braunschweig-Lüneburg

101. (Cat. No. 63) A HANSEATIC MERCHANT, THE SO-CALLED GOLDSMITH HANS OF ANTWERP. 1532/33
London, Victoria and Albert Museum (Salting Bequest)

ANNO.1532.   ÆTATIS.SVÆ.29

103. (Cat. No. 65) HERMANN WEDIGH, MERCHANT OF COLOGNE. 1532. New York, Metropolitan Museum

ANNO 1533

ÆTATIS SVÆ 39

104. (Cat. No. 66) HERMANN-HILLEBRANDT WEDIGH, MERCHANT OF COLOGNE. 1533. Berlin, Deutsches Museum

105. (Cat. No. 67) DIRK TYBIS, MERCHANT OF DUISBURG. 1533. Vienna, Kunsthistorisches Museum

106. (Cat. No. 68) THE HANSEATIC MERCHANT CYRIACUS KALE. 1533. Brunswick, Herzog-Anton-Ulrich-Museum

DERICHVS SI VOCEAT ADDAS IPSISSIMVS HIC
HVNC DVBITES PICTOR FECERIT AN GENITO
DER BORN ETATIS SVÆ·23 ANNO 1535

107. (Cat. No. 69) DERICH BORN, MERCHANT OF COLOGNE. 1533. Windsor Castle
Reproduced by gracious permission of His Majesty The King

108. (Cat. No. 71) JOHN (OR WILLIAM) RESKIMER OF MURTHYR. About 1533. Windsor Castle

Reproduced by gracious permission of His Majesty The King

ROBERTVS CHESEMAN .
ANNO   DM

ETATES.SVÆ XLVIII·
M D XXXIII

109. (Cat. No. 72) ROBERT CHESEMAN OF DORMANSWELL, "THE FALCONER OF KING HENRY VIII". 1533. The Hague, Mauritshuis
110. On opposite page. HAWK. Detail from Plate 109

III. (Cat. No. 73) SIR NICHOLAS CAREW, EQUERRY TO KING HENRY VIII. 1532/33
Drumlanrig Castle, Thornhill, Scotland, Duke of Buccleuch

112. HEAD OF SIR NICHOLAS CAREW. Detail from Plate III

113. (Cat. No. 74) THE FRENCH AMBASSADORS: JEAN DE DINTEVILLE, LORD OF POLISY, AND GEORGES DE SELVE, BISHOP OF LAVOUR. 1533
London, National Gallery

114. HEAD OF JEAN DE DINTEVILLE. Detail from Plate 113

116. JEAN DE DINTEVILLE'S RIGHT HAND ON A DAGGER WITH A CHASED GOLD SHEATH. Detail from Plate 113

117. (Cat. No. 70) THE MERCHANT DERICH BORN OF COLOGNE. 1533
(cf. Plate 107). Munich, Alte Pinakothek

118. (Cat. No. 77) YOUNG MAN WITH CARNATION. 1533. Upton House, Banbury, Estate of Lord Bearsted

119. (Cat. No. 76) SIR HENRY GUILDFORD. About 1533
Detroit, Institute of Arts

120. (Cat. No. 80) A COURT OFFICIAL OF KING HENRY VIII,
PROBABLY THE PAINTER LUCAS HOREBOUT. About 1534
Formerly Ripaille Castle, Lake Geneva, Collection Engel-Gros

121–122. (Cat. No. 78-79) A COURT OFFICIAL OF KING HENRY VIII, AND HIS WIFE. 1534. Vienna, Kunsthistorisches Museum

123. (Cat. No. 82) WOMAN WITH WHITE LINEN COIF. About 1534. Detroit, Mrs. Edsel B. Ford

124. (Cat. No. 83) RICHARD MABON, DEACON OF THE PARISH OF ST. HELIER ON THE ISLE OF JERSEY. About 1534
Enschede, Holland, Rijksmuseum Twenthe

125. (Cat. No. 81) THOMAS CROMWELL, MASTER OF THE JEWEL HOUSE. 1534. New York, Frick Collection

126. HEAD OF THOMAS CROMWELL. Detail from Plate 125

127. (Cat. No. 84) UNKNOWN GENTLEMAN WITH MUSIC-BOOKS AND A LUTE. 1534/6. Berlin, Deutsches Museum

128. (Cat. No. 86) UNKNOWN GENTLEMAN, HOLDING GLOVES. 1535. New York, Metropolitan Museum (Bache Collection)

129. (Cat. No. 85) CHARLES DE SOLIER, SIR DE MORETTE, FRENCH AMBASSADOR TO THE ENGLISH COURT
1535. Dresden, Staatliche Gemäldegalerie

130. (Cat. No. 87) DERICH BERCK, MERCHANT OF COLOGNE. 1536. New York, Metropolitan Museum (Bache Collection)

X° IVLII. ANNO.
H. VIII. XXVIII.°

ETATIS · SVÆ
ANNO XXXIII.

131. (Cat. No. 88) SIR RICHARD SOUTHWELL. 1536. Florence, Uffizi

132. (Cat. No. 89) SIR THOMAS LE STRANGE. 1536. Private Collection in America

133. (Cat. No. 91) SIR JOHN GODSALVE, SITTING ON A WOODEN BENCH. About 1536. Philadelphia, John Johnson Collection

134. (Cat. No. 92) ELIZABETH WIDMERPOLE, SIR JOHN GODSALVE'S WIFE, SITTING ON A WOODEN BENCH. About 1536.
Winterthur, Collection Oskar Reinhart

135. (Cat. No. 94) KING HENRY VIII. 1536 (Pendant to Plate 136). Lugano, Baron Thyssen's Family Bequest

136. (Cat. No. 95) QUEEN JANE SEYMOUR, KING HENRY VIII'S THIRD WIFE. 1536 (Pendant to Plate 135)
The Hague, Mauritshuis

137. (Cat. No. 96) KING HENRY VIII. 1537 (Replica). Windsor Castle
Reproduced by gracious permission of His Majesty The King

138. (Cat. No. 97) JANE SEYMOUR, KING HENRY VIII'S THIRD WIFE. 1536. Vienna, Kunsthistorisches Museum

139. (Cat. No. 98) CHRISTINA OF DENMARK, DUCHESS OF MILAN. 1538. London, National Gallery

140. (Cat. No. 99) HEAD OF CHRISTINA OF DENMARK. Detail from Plate 139

141. (Cat. No. 100) UNKNOWN GENTLEMAN WITH A BLACK BERET. 1538. Geneva, Private Collection

142. (Cat. No. 101) A HANSEATIC MERCHANT. 1538. New York, Dr. Hamilton Rice

143. (Cat. No. 102) CHARLES BRANDON, DUKE OF SUFFOLK. 1540/41. Formerly London, Norbert Fischman Gallery

144. (Cat. No. 103) THOMAS HOWARD, DUKE OF NORFOLK. 1538/39. Windsor Castle

Reproduced by gracious permission of His Majesty The King

145. (Cat. No. 104) SIMON GEORGE OF QUOCOTE. About 1540. Frankfurt, Staedelsches Institut

PARVVLE PATRISSA, PATRIÆ VIRTVTIS ET HÆRES
  ESTO, NIHIL MAIVS MAXIMVS ORBIS HABET.
GNATVM VIX POSSVNT COELVM ET NATVRA DEDISSE,
  HVIVS QVEM PATRIS, VICTVS HONORET HONOS.
ÆQVATO TANTVM, TANTI TV FACTA PARENTIS,
  VOTA HOMINVM, VIX QVO PROGRFDIANTVR, HABENT
VINCITO, VICISTI. QVOT REGES PRISCVS ADORAT
  ORBIS, NEC TE QVI VINCERE POSSIT, ERIT.

146. (Cat. No. 105) EDWARD, PRINCE OF WALES. 1539. Washington, National Gallery of Art (Mellon Collection)

ANNO · ÆTATIS ·   · SVÆ · XLIX ·

147. (Cat. No. 106) KING HENRY VIII IN WEDDING DRESS. 1539/40 (Replica). Rome, National Gallery

148. (Cat. No. 107) QUEEN ANNE OF CLEVES, FOURTH WIFE OF KING HENRY VIII, IN WEDDING DRESS. 1539/40
Paris, Musée du Louvre

149. (Cat. No. 110) UNKNOWN LADY OF THE COURT OF HENRY VIII. 1540/43. New York, Metropolitan Museum (Bache Collection)

150. (Cat. No. 111) UNKNOWN ENGLISH LADY. 1540/43. Vienna, Kunsthistorisches Museum

ETATIS · SVÆ · 34 ·

151. (Cat. No. 112) MARGARET WYATT, LADY LEE. About 1540. New York, Metropolitan Museum

152. (Cat. No. 113) UNKNOWN GENTLEMAN, HOLDING HIS GLOVES AND A LETTER. About 1540
Basle, Öffentliche Kunstsammlung

ANNO· ·1541·

·ETATIS· ·SVÆ·37·

153. (Cat. No. 114) A MEMBER OF THE DUTCH FAMILY VOS VAN STEENWIJK. 1541. Berlin, Deutsches Museum

ANNO · DÑI · 1541 ·   ETATIS · SVÆ · 2 8 ·

154. (Cat. No. 115) UNKNOWN YOUNG MAN AT HIS OFFICE DESK. 1541. Vienna, Kunsthistorisches Museum

155. (Cat. No. 116) UNKNOWN YOUNG GIRL WITH WHITE COIF. 1541
Los Angeles, County Museum

156. (Cat. No. 117) LADY ELIZABETH RICH. 1541/43. Basle, Nathan Katz Gallery

157. (Cat. No. 118) QUEEN CATHERINE HOWARD, FIFTH WIFE OF KING HENRY VIII. 1540/41
Toledo, U.S.A., Museum of Art

158. (Cat. No. 119) KING HENRY VIII IN A WIDE VELVET SURCOAT. 1542. Castle Howard, York, George Howard Esq.

159. HEAD OF KING HENRY VIII. Detail from Plate 158

160. RIGHT UPPER SLEEVE, EMBROIDERED WITH PEARLS AND DECORATED WITH THREE BEJEWELLED GOLD SPANGLES
Detail from Plate 158

161. (Cat. No. 122) THE POET HENRY HOWARD, EARL OF SURREY. 1542/43. New York, Wildenstein & Co. Inc.

162. (Cat. No. 121) UNKNOWN ENGLISH NOBLEMAN WITH A HAWK. 1542. The Hague, Mauritshuis

163. (Cat. No. 120) SIR GEORGE CAREW. About 1543. Weston Park, Shifnal, England, Earl of Bradford

164. (Cat. No. 123) SIR WILLIAM BUTTS THE YOUNGER. 1543. Boston, Museum of Fine Arts

165. (Cat. No. 124) SIR WILLIAM BUTTS, PHYSICIAN TO KING HENRY VIII. About 1543 (Pendant to Plate 166)
Boston, Isabella Stewart Gardner Museum

ANNO ÆTATIS SVÆ·LVII

166. (Cat. No. 125) LADY MARGARET BUTTS. About 1543 (Pendant to Plate 165)
Boston, Isabella Stewart Gardner Museum

ÆTATIS ·   SVE ◄ 88 ◄

167. (Cat. No. 126) DR. JOHN CHAMBERS, PHYSICIAN TO KING HENRY VIII. About 1543. Vienna, Kunsthistorisches Museum

ÆTATIS · · SVÆ · 54 ·

168. (Cat. No. 127) ANTON THE GOOD, DUKE OF LORRAINE. 1543. Berlin, Deutsches Museum

ÆTATIS   S VÆ · VI ·

169. (Cat. No. 128) EDWARD, PRINCE OF WALES, AT THE AGE OF SIX YEARS. 1543
New York, Metropolitan Museum (Bache Collection)

170. (Cat. No. 129) PRINCESS MARY, DAUGHTER OF KING HENRY VIII. 1543
London, Private Collection

171. (Cat. No. 130) SELF-PORTRAIT OF THE ARTIST. 1542/43
Indianapolis, U.S.A., Dr. G. A. H. Clowes

MINIATURES

172. (Cat. No. 132) BEARDED YOUNG MAN WITH RED BERET. About 1534/35. Paris, M. Leo Michelsen

173. (Cat. No. 147) A BOY IN A BROWN DOUBLET. About 1540. The Hague, Royal Archives

174. (Cat. No. 140) MRS. PEMBERTON. About 1540. London, Victoria and Albert Museum

175–176. (Cat. No. 134–135) WILLIAM ROPER OF WELLHALL AND HIS WIFE MARGARET MORE. 1536
New York, Mrs. Henry Goldman

177. (Cat. No. 138) THOMAS WRIOTHESLEY, EARL OF SOUTHAMPTON. 1538. New York, Metropolitan Museum

178

179

180

181

178. (Cat. No. 139) QUEEN ANNE OF CLEVES. 1539/40 (cf. Plate 148)
London, Victoria and Albert Museum (Salting Bequest)

179–180. (Cat. No. 141–142) QUEEN CATHERINE HOWARD. 1540/42 (cf. Plate 157)
(179) Windsor Castle. (180) Drumlanrig Castle, Thornhill, Scotland, Duke of Buccleuch

181. (Cat. No. 143) LADY ELIZABETH AUDLEY. After 1540. Windsor Castle

179 and 181: *Reproduced by gracious permission of His Majesty The King*

182. (Cat. No. 144) THE PAINTER HARRY MAYNERT. After 1540. Munich, Bavarian National Museum

183–184. (Cat. No. 145–146) HENRY AND CHARLES BRANDON, SONS OF THE DUKE OF SUFFOLK. 1541. Windsor Castle
Reproduced by gracious permission of His Majesty The King

185. (Cat. No. 148) HEINRICH VON SCHWARZWALD, MERCHANT OF DANZIG. 1543. Danzig, Stadtmuseum

186. (Cat. No. 149) SELF-PORTRAIT OF THE ARTIST. 1543. London, Wallace Collection

187. (Cat. No. 150) SELF-PORTRAIT OF THE ARTIST. 1543. Drumlanrig Castle, Thornhill, Scotland, Duke of Buccleuch

188. (Cat. No. 151) SELF-PORTRAIT OF THE ARTIST. 1543. Antwerp, Mayer van den Bergh Museum

189

190

191

189. (Cat. No. 133) GEORGE NEVILL, LORD ABERGAVENNY. After 1534
Drumlanrig Castle, Thornhill, Scotland, Duke of Buccleuch

190–191. (Cat. No. 137) THOMAS CROMWELL, EARL OF ESSEX. About 1538. (cf. Plate 125). London, Art Dealer

MONUMENTAL AND DECORATIVE PAINTINGS

192. CENTRE PART OF THE TABLE PAINTED FOR HANS BAER OF BASLE, WITH THE ALLIANCE ARMS, ST. NOBODY, AND THE SLEEPING PEDLAR ROBBED BY MONKEYS. Detail from Plate 193

193. (Cat. No. 152) PAINTED TABLE-TOP FOR HANS BAER AND HI

UNNER, OF BASLE. 1515. Zurich, Schweizerisches Landesmuseum

195. CATCHING BIRDS AND CAPTURING GIRLS. Detail from Plate 193

Wer Jemandt hie der gern wölt lernen dütsch schriben und läsen
uß dem aller kürtzisten grundt den Jeman erdencken kan Do durch
ein Jeder der vor nit ein büchstabem kan · Der mag kürtzlich und bald
begriffen ein grundt do durch er mag von im selbs lernen sin schuld
uff schribe vnd läsen vnd wer es nit gelernen kan so vngeschickt
were Den will ich vm nut vnd vergeben gelert habm vnd gantz nut
von im zü lon nemen es sig wer es well burger oder hantwercks ge
sellen frouwen vnd junckfrouwen wer sin bedarff der kum har in der
wirt drüwlich gelert vm ein zimlichen lon · Aber die junge Knabe
vnd meitlin noch den fronuasten · wie gewonheit ist · 1 5 1 6 ·

wer jemand hie der gern wölt lernen tütsch schriben und läsen uß dem aller kurtzisten grundt den jeman erdencken kan do durch en jeder der vor nit ein buchstaben kan der mag kürtzlich und bald begriffen ein grundt Do durch er mag von jm selber lernen sin schuld uff schriben und läsen · und wer es nit getrauwen kan so ungeschickt wer den will ich um nüt und um ur= geben gelert haben und gantz nüt von jm zu lon nemen er syg · wer er well burger oder handwercks gesellen frowen und ju= nkfrouwen · wer sin bedarff der kum har jn · der wirt drüwlich gelert um ein zimlichen lon · Aber die jungen knaben und mei tlin noch den fronvasten wie gewonheit ist · Anno · M · cccc · xvi

197. (Cat. No. 154) REVERSE OF THE SIGN-BOARD OF THE SCHOOLMASTER OSWALD MYCONIUS. 1516. Basle, Öffentliche Kunstsammlung

198. (Cat. No. 158) "THE DEATH OF LUCRETIA", LUCRETIA'S HUSBAND. 1517
Fragment of the fresco mural on the façade of the Hertenstein House in Lucerne
Lucerne, Kunstmuseum

199. (Cat. No. 155) PRINTER'S MARK OF JOHANNES FROBEN. 1523. Basle, Öffentliche Kunstsammlung

200. (Cat. No. 156) THE EMPEROR HENRY II, HIS WIFE KUNIGUNDE AND THE MINSTER OF BASLE

Inside of the left shutter of the organ doors, formerly in the Basle Minster. 1525/26. Basle, Öffentliche Kunstsammlung

201. (Cat. No. 157) THE VIRGIN AND CHILD, ST. PANTALUS, FIRST BISHOP OF BASLE, AND NUDE ANGEL MUSICIANS
Inside of the right shutter of the organ doors, formerly in the Basle Minster. 1525/26. Basle, Öffentliche Kunstsammlung

202. HEAD OF EMPEROR HENRY II. Detail from Plate 200

203. VIRGIN AND CHILD. Detail from Plate 201

204–205. (Cat. No. 169) HEADS OF CHARONDAS AND OF A FRIGHTENED SPECTATOR. 1522
Fragments of the fresco mural "THE DEATH OF CHARONDAS"
Formerly in the Council Chamber of the Basle Town Hall. Basle, Öffentliche Kunstsammlung

206. (Cat. No. 171) HEADS OF "THE SAMNITE AMBASSADORS BEFORE MARCUS CURTIUS DENTATUS". 1522
Fragment of the fresco mural
Formerly in the Council Chamber of the Basle Town Hall. Basle, Öffentliche Kunstsammlung

207–210. (Cat. No. 172) SIX HEADS. 1530. Four Fragments of the fresco mural "KING REHOBOAM REBUKING THE ELDERS"
Formerly in the Council Chamber of the Basle Town Hall. Basle, Öffentliche Kunstsammlung

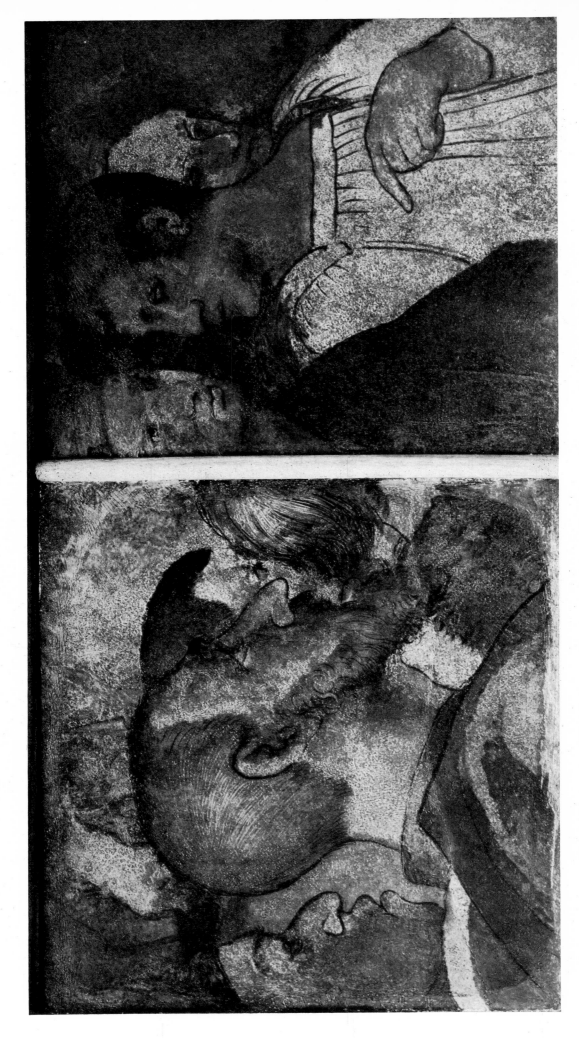

211–212. (Cat. No. 172) HEADS OF COUNCILLORS AND ELDERS. 1530. Fragments of the fresco mural. "KING REHOBOAM REBUKING THE ELDERS"
Formerly in the Council Chamber of the Basle Town Hall. Basle, Öffentliche Kunstsammlung

213. (Cat. No. 172) THE KING. 1530. Fragment of the fresco mural "KING REHOBOAM REBUKING THE ELDERS"
Formerly in the Council Chamber of the Basle Town Hall. Basle, Öffentliche Kunstsammlung

214. (Cat. No. 179) KING HENRY VIII AND HIS FATHER. 1537
Cartoon (left part) of the lost fresco mural in Whitehall. Chatsworth, Duke of Devonshire

215. HEAD OF KING HENRY VII. Detail from Plate 214

216. HEAD OF KING HENRY VIII. Detail from Plate 214

217. (Cat. No. 180) SOLOMON AND THE QUEEN OF SHEBA. Miniature painting, probably design for a mural decoration. Windsor Castle

Reproduced by gracious permission of His Majesty The King

218. (Cat. No. 181) KING HENRY VIII GRANTING A CHARTER OF INCORPORATION TO THE BARBER-SURGEONS' COMPANY. 1542/43. London, Barber-Surgeons' Hall

219. (Cat. No. 181) THE BARBER-SURGEONS' PICTURE. REPLICA WITH A WINDOW. London, Royal College of Surgeons

220. (Cat. No. 181) KING HENRY VIII. Detail from Plate 218

CATALOGUE

NOTE TO THE CATALOGUE

THE IDENTIFICATION of the earliest works of Hans Holbein the Younger is not yet complete although, thanks to the investigations of *Ernst Buchner* and *Ludwig von Baldass*, our knowledge of the elder Holbein's work has been greatly increased (*Augsburger Kunst der Spätgotik und Renaissance, Augsburg 1928*). The activity of the workshop founded in Augsburg in 1490 by Hans Holbein the Elder was considerable; apart from his brother Sigmund and his two sons Ambros and Hans the Younger, various journeymen painters, including Leonhard Beck, also worked there. The characteristic features of the elder Hans's art such as a careful observation of nature, a direct grasp of people and their actions as well as a purely decorative use of Renaissance motives, give their stamp to the workshop production and recur in the authentic works of the two sons. For that reason it is not easy to distinguish between their work during the years 1515–1517. Sigmund Holbein, of whom no authentic work is known, refused to accompany his brother Hans when the latter moved to Isenheim; shortly after he must have gone to Switzerland, where he settled down in Berne. By 1513–14 the two sons had already left their father's workshop and had worked their way via Constance to Basle, where they were employed as journeymen painters by Hans Herbster. It seems to me not improbable that from time to time the members of the family were once more united in some common task such as, for example, the decoration of the Hertenstein house in Lucerne. A sketch for the Legend of the fourteen Holy Helpers for the wall-painting in Lucerne in the father's sketch book would indicate that the elder Hans, who left Augsburg in 1517, collaborated in Lucerne. The less characteristic paintings do not allow of a critical distinction between the various hands but they do show clearly the rather uneven nature of the represen-

Three portrait studies in the Öffentliche Kunstsammlung, Basle

BY HANS HOLBEIN THE ELDER   BY HANS HOLBEIN THE YOUNGER   BY AMBROSIUS HOLBEIN

tational style, open to various influences, which is typical of the early works of Hans Holbein the Younger. Recently, thanks to Mr. Ludwig Goldscheider, the belief in young Hans's left-handedness has been revived, a view already upheld by Carel van Mander in his book: *Het Leven der doorluchtighe Nederlandtsche en Hooghduytsche Schilders* in the 1618 edition and by Sandrart in his *Academie der Bau-, Bild- und Mahlerey-Künste* of 1675, which has made it easier to distinguish between the drawings. This is of capital importance in determining Hans Holbein's part in the marginal drawings for the 'Praise of Folly' and upholds the tradition which had been challenged by *H. A. Schmid*.

Frequent borrowing of motives from contemporary artists occurs both in the work of the father and of the sons; they also used the same models, sculptures and etchings, so that the same work is attributed now to the one now to the other. Hans is early recognizable by a sober objectivity and artistic superiority but he was not able to develop his own particular style until after his visit to Lombardy.

ABBREVIATIONS

Chamberlain = Arthur B. Chamberlain, Hans Holbein the Younger. 2 vols. London, 1913.

KdK. = Klassiker der Kunst in Gesamtausgaben, vol. 20. Hans Holbein d.J. Edited by Paul Ganz. Stuttgart, 1912.

Ganz, C. R. = Die Handzeichnungen Hans Holbein des Jüngeren, Kritischer Katalog der Facsimile-Ausgabe, 1937.

Parker, W.Dr. = The Drawings of Hans Holbein in the Collection of His Majesty the King at Windsor Castle, by K. T. Parker. London, 1945.

P. = Gustav Parthey, Wenzel Hollar, Beschreibendes Verzeichnis seiner Kupferstiche. Berlin, 1853.

W. = Alfred Woltmann, Holbein und seine Zeit. Second revised edition, 2 vols. Leipzig, 1874-76.

CATALOGUE OF THE PAINTINGS

I. RELIGIOUS PAINTINGS

1. THE HOLY VIRGIN ENTHRONED IN GLORY, ADORED BY ANGELS. Dated: MDXIIII. Tempera on limewood. 14½ × 11¾. *Basle, Öffentliche Kunstsammlung.* PLATE 1

The English translation of the two-line Latin inscription on the parapet of the Renaissance structure is: 'She, who gave birth as a maid and remained a maid, fed God with her own breast and bore him safely in trembling arms past all obstacles.' The two Italian escutcheons on either side of the Virgin's head show the coats-of-arms of Botzheim and Ycker von Beringen, the parents of John von Botzheim, canon of Constance, the donor of the panel. The latter, said by Erasmus (*Hegner 125*) to be an art-loving clergyman well known as a collector of pictures and books, was, according to the 'Zimmerische Chronik', a doctor of Law and had studied for a long time in Italy.

Today the picture is attributed to Ambros Holbein although the natural conception of mother and child and a similar silverpoint drawing (*Ganz, C. R. 101*) as well as the skilfully constructed Renaissance building, an Italian motive to be found in Mantegna's work ('Virgin and Child', Berlin, Kaiser Friedrich Museum), seem rather to indicate Hans. The letters RA–CA appear on one of the small panels held by the angels and also a monogram that Chamberlain thought he could decipher as AH or HH. He regarded C.A. as an abbreviation for *Civis Augustanus* (citizen of Augsburg).

2. VIRGIN AND CHILD UNDER A RENAISSANCE PORCH. Signed and dated: HANS HOLBEIN 1515. Oil and tempera on pinewood. 19¼ × 13⅜. *London, Art Dealer.* PLATE 2 (3)

The figure group is taken from a painting of the Virgin by the elder Hans which came to the Vienna gallery from the Kaufmann collection in Berlin (illustrated in *Beiträge zur Geschichte der deutschen Kunst, vol. 3 II, p. 173*); the architectural frame is derived from an Italian sculpture and was used on more than one occasion by the Augsburg sculptor Hans Daucher for reliefs with representations of the Virgin (cf. *Ph.M. Halm, Studien zur süddeutschen Plastik, vol. II, p. 189 ff.: Hans Daucher. Augsburg, 1927*) and by Hans Holbein the Elder in his picture 'The Fountain of Life' in Lisbon as the central point of the composition. The filling of the arch opening, the small panel containing Holbein's name, is borrowed from an engraving by Nicoletto da Modena, and other motives are copied from Zoan Andrea. In 1921 the picture was found to be heavily overpainted. Judging by the notices and seals on the back, it must at one time have been in a royal Bavarian collection; during the first half of the

nineteenth century it was in the collections of Metzler and Johannes von Müller at Schaffhausen and later in that of Moreau Wolsey in Paris. Finally it turned up in England and in 1921 belonged to Mr. L. Gow in London. *Woltmann* mentions it as a lost work by Hans Holbein the Elder (*II, No. 288*). (cf. *P. Ganz, Ein Jugendwerk Hans Holbein d. J. in Jahrbuch für Kunst und Kunstpflege in der Schweiz 1915–21 p. 366 ff.*)

3. THE PROCESSION TO CALVARY. Signed: H. H. 1515. Oil and tempera on pinewood. 29⅜ × 56⅛. *Karlsruhe, Staatliche Kunsthalle.* PLATE 4 (5)

First work to be signed with initials. Various motives, in the first place the group of Christ surrounded by men, St. Veronica (not represented again by Holbein in a later 'Procession to Calvary') and the coarse and rather sketchily painted 'Crowning of Thorns' on a black ground on the reverse side are taken from the Vetter votive picture by the elder Hans. The head in profile on the right above the cross is a portrait of the humanist Sebastian Brandt, of whom Burgkmair painted a portrait in profile (Karlsruhe, Staatliche Kunsthalle). The crude and hasty painting on the back is so badly damaged that it is no longer possible to establish its authenticity.

The painting originated in Basle and came later to the Basle court of the Margrave of Baden, where it was entered in the inventory of 1773 as a work by Holbein in the Display room. Since the publication of *Lübke's* views in the *Repertorium für Kunstwissenschaft, vol. 10*, it is generally acknowledged to be a work by the younger Holbein (cf. also *Saxl, Belvedere 9 June 1930, pp. 205–15*); but various writers, for instance *H. Koegler* and *U. Christoffel* maintain that the monogram should be read as Hans Herbster, of whom, however, no acknowledged work is known.

4–6. THREE SCENES FROM THE PASSION OF CHRIST. 1515–17. PLATES 6, 7, 9

The following three scenes belong to a Passion series painted on canvas of which five paintings and a preliminary drawing for 'Christ carrying the Cross' have survived. They show the work of various hands and in all probability originated in Hans Herbster's workshop, where the brothers Ambros and Hans worked as journeyman painters during the first year of their stay in Basle. The sketches all appear to be by Hans Holbein; the quality of the finished work, however, is so uneven that two of the paintings, 'The Arrest' and 'Pilate

(215)

washing his Hands' cannot even be considered as works
by the two Holbeins.

The 'Last Supper' and 'The Scourging' come from the
Amerbach print-room where they are entered in the
inventory of 1586 as 'Hans Holbeins erste arbeiten eine
auf tuch mit ölfarb' (Hans Holbein's first works in oil on
canvas); the remaining three scenes were bought at the
Birmann sale in 1836.

Motives taken from Dürer's 'Little Passion' (cf. *KdK.*,
p. 283, 21–25) and the lack of direct Italian influence
suggest the first stay in Basle as the date of the series.

4. The Last Supper, in the background Christ washing the Disciples' feet. Tempera on canvas.
56 × 60⅛. *Basle, Öffentliche Kunstsammlung (Amerbach-Kabinett)*.   PLATE 6

The Renaissance motives in the architecture have the
same prototypes as Holbein's earliest book-titles. The
pillared portico with its barrel-vaulted, coffered ceiling
over the 'Washing of the Feet' is already to be found in
the Madonna of 1515 and in the double portrait of the
burgomaster Meyer and his wife of 1516. Several heads
show the influence of Grünewald.

5. The Agony in the Garden and the Betrayal of Judas
(according to St. John xviii, 3). Tempera on
canvas, 51¾ × 51¾. *Basle, Öffentliche Kunstsammlung*.
                                                  PLATE 7 (8)

In the background on the right is the silhouette of the
cathedral of Basle. The landscape is related to the one by
Grünewald on the Isenheim altar.

6. The Scourging of Christ. Tempera on canvas.
54 × 45⅛. *Basle, Öffentliche Kunstsammlung (Amerbach-Kabinett)*.   PLATE 9

The picture contains motives from Baldung's 'Crucifixion' of 1516 in Aschaffenburg, from one of Dürer's
etchings of the 'Little Passion' of 1512 and from Holbein's
own 'Procession to Calvary' of 1515 at Karlsruhe (dress
of the soldier on the right).

7–8. Heads of two Saints. About 1515. Tempera on
pinewood. 9¼ × 8½. *Basle, Öffentliche Kunstsammlung
(Amerbach-Kabinett)*.   PLATES 10–11

The fragments, of which the male figure could be a St.
John the evangelist, are listed in the inventory of the
Amerbach print-room as the earliest works of Hans
Holbein: 'Item Heads of a young Saint and Virgin with
Patenen on Wood with Oil Colour small. H. Holbein
first work.'

9. Adam tempted by Eve. Signed and dated: 1517 H.H.
Tempera on paper mounted on pinewood. 11⅜ × 14.
Basle, Öffentliche Kunstsammlung (Amerbach-Kabinett).
                                                  PLATE 12

The same models were used for the two heads as for the
heads of the saints of 1515 and they show the influence
of Baldung and Dürer.

10. Altar-piece with Scenes from the Passion of Christ.
Formerly in the St. Francis or 'Barfüsser' church
at Lucerne. 1518/19. Size of one table 46⅛ × 22½ (after a
copy in Palermo).   FIG. 1–2

The five scenes listed by Patin in his 'Index Operum
Holbenii', 1676, may have formed the shutters, painted
on both sides, and the predella of the altar, which at that
time was still with the Augustinian monks. The altar
has disappeared but a 'Lamentation at the foot of the
Cross' has been preserved in seven different copies. A
comparison with the Oberried altar three years later
suggests that the outer sides of the shutters may have
represented on the left the 'Nativity' with the adoring
parents and the 'Annunciation to the Shepherds', and
on the right the 'Adoration of the Magi'. The inner sides
showed the twelve-year-old Christ teaching in the temple
and the 'Lamentation after the Descent from the Cross'.

The latter has been preserved in copies which give an
indication of the size of the altar-piece (the copy in
Palermo is 46⅛ × 22½). The motive of the two angels
holding the sudary of St. Veronica presumably adorned
the predella; the central panel can no longer be deter-
mined unless we suppose it to be the 'Christ on the Cross
between Mary and John', the sixth picture of the Patin
inventory. A copy of an early work by Holbein representing the same scene was formerly in the Amerbach-
Kabinett and is now in the Öffentliche Kunstsammlung
in Basle (ill. *KdK., p. 188.*)

It is strange that only one scene of the altarpiece should
have been copied. But in point of fact copies of the
'Lamentation' have so far alone been identified. These
are in Palermo (*KdK., p. 187*), in a private collection in
London (*Burlington Fine Arts Club 1906, Catalogue of Early
German Art, p. XL*), in Lucerne (sacristy of the church of
St. Francis) and in Baden, Aargau (as a station of the
cross in the city church). A traced copy in the print-room
of the Basle museum, made by the Basle painter Jerome
Hess in 1834 from the copy sold by Marquard
Wocher to England, measures only 17½ × 8⅞. The same
painting was copied in 1648, when it was still in the
church, by the Zürich painter Konrad Meyer in a pen
drawing with colour indications (Kunsthaus Zurich, formerly Ganz collection), and the group of the 'Virgin with
the dead Christ', with the sides reversed, by the mono-
gramist H.H.W., probably the painter Hans Heinrich
Wegman of Lucerne (died 1628). (See *P. Ganz, Handzeichnungen Schweizerischer Meister, vol. 3, Plate 45.*) An
early drawing by Holbein in the Augsburg museum,
representing Christ on the Cross with Mary, John and
Mary Magdalen, is closely related in style. (*Ganz, C.R.
102.*)

As Patin mentions only the subjects and says nothing
about the form of the altar-piece, it is possible that the
pictures were placed in a richly carved and gilded architectural frame in the Lombard fashion—a solution that
might also be considered for the shutters of the Passion.

FIG. 1 (Cat. No. 10). Copy in Palermo

FIG. 2 (Cat. No. 10). After two drawings by Konrad Meyer

11–12. CHRIST AS MAN OF SORROWS AND THE VIRGIN AS MATER DOLOROSA. 1519/20. Tempera on limewood. Each 11½ × 7⅝. *Basle, Öffentliche Kunstsammlung (Amerbach-Kabinett).* PLATES 13–14

The small panels painted in brown monochrome with a pale blue sky formed a diptych such as was customary in the Gothic Period. The same technique 'in false colours' is to be found in the sketch of the 'Holy Family in front of a Renaissance porch', executed about the same time (*Ganz, C. R. 106*), in the print-room in Basle. Equally complicated architectural compositions are frequently seen on Holbein's early glass designs; the individual motives are taken from Lombard buildings, in particular the cathedral of Como (Porta della Rana). The figure of Christ is similarly conceived in a drawing dated 1519 in the print-room in Berlin (*Ganz, C.R. 466* and *Auswahl von Handzeichnungen Hans Holbeins d.J., Basle 1943*).

13. THE LAST SUPPER AFTER LEONARDO DA VINCI. About 1520. Oil and tempera on limewood. 45½ × 38⅜ (original size, 59 × 59). *Basle, Öffentliche Kunstsammlung (Amerbach-Kabinett).* PLATE 15

The altarpiece, described in the Amerbach inventory as badly slashed and stuck together again, is roughly cut down on both sides and along the top; three of the apostles and the upper termination of the architecture are missing. In the centre a square piece with Christ and a portion of John has been sawn out and re-inserted later.

The composition is copied from Leonardo's wall painting in the Refectory of S. Maria delle Grazie in Milan. The figure of Christ with the dominating gesture of the hands has been retained almost unchanged by Holbein as the central point but the groups of three of the apostles have been compressed to suit the size of the panel. The pillared hall with the three openings in the background show no perspective depths as they do in Leonardo's work. The rear wall of the room was raised, probably by an archway, that corresponded to the upper sections of the shutters with the eight passion scenes. The branches of the fig tree, the curtains and the house on the right are Holbein's own additions as well as the halo in the shape of a small ring floating above the head of the Saviour which recurs on the one Passion shutter and on the Oberried altarpiece, but not again.

The panel must have been painted shortly after Holbein's return from Italy, at the same time as the Passion of Christ (*Cat. No. 10*); the impressions received in Lombardy are directly apparent in the build-up of the composition, in the borrowing of Italian motives, in the colouring and in the new technique of painting. Stylistically the 'Passion' is most nearly akin to the Lucerne panel (Catalogue No. 10). According to Peter Ochs, the panel was from the first destined for the town hall but other suppositions and traditions assume that it was brought to the town hall for safety during the iconoclastic storms, when it may have been forcibly extracted from the frame and damaged in the process. At a council meeting in 1770 it was decided to have the painting transferred to the art collection and in 1771 it was badly restored by Nicolas Groot. Two old copies in the Basle art collection may possibly show the original condition of the picture. According to *H. A. Schmid*, who attempted a reconstruction of the altarpiece, the shutters with the 'Last Supper' and the 'Passion' were not done until 1524/25 (cf. *H. A. Schmid, Die Werke Hans Holbeins in Basel, Öffentliche Kunstsammlung, Kleiner Führer No. 2, 1930*).

14. THE PASSION OF CHRIST. About 1520. Oil and tempera on limewood. Four panels, the shutters of an altar-piece(?). Total measurements in its present form $59\frac{1}{8} \times 58\frac{1}{4}$. Individual measurements $26\frac{3}{4}$–$29\frac{7}{8} \times 13$. *Basle, Öffentliche Kunstsammlung.*   PLATE 16 (17–30)

If the panels, which are painted on one side only, did not form an altar-piece by themselves, it can be assumed that the central panel was formed by the 'Last Supper' (Catalogue No. 13) whose measurements when complete correspond to the total measurements of the shutters. There are strong reminiscences of Italian painting, in particular of Mantegna and the Lombard artists, from whom Holbein had learnt to use a thin coating of paint and an enamel-like lustre of the colours.

Single Italian motives to be noted are the figure of Caiphas enthroned and the warrior with the spear in the foreground of the 'Crucifixion' who is derived from Mantegna; the 'Entombment' group, too, is reminiscent of Raphael's famous painting of 1507 for Perugia (Rome, Galleria Borghese). Another stimulus from Italian art is to be seen in the strong light effects; a comparison between the procession of the bailiffs in the 'Agony in the Garden' with the corresponding group from the first Passion series shows, for example, how the narrative style of the latter work has given way to a desire for greater pictorial light

effects, a conception which, however, gradually recedes with Holbein during the course of the next few years. The Romanesque architecture in the 'Scourging' is inspired by the church of Othmarsheim in Upper Alsace. The eight scenes are painted on four upright panels, on the reverse sides of which a few colour samples are to be seen. The fact that the panels are painted on one side only permits the assumption that the pictures were not used as wings, but were framed as a sequence in a Renaissance frame.

15. CHRIST IN THE TOMB. Signed and dated: MDXXI. H.H. Oil and tempera on limewood. $12 \times 78\frac{3}{4}$. *Basle, Öffentliche Kunstsammlung (Amerbach-Kabinett)*. PLATE 31 (32–34)

The representation of the dead Christ on the predella was seen by Holbein on Grünewald's Isenheim altar, where Christ is lying next to the sarcophagus, supported by John and mourned by the Marys. In the second version, too, which Grünewald painted for the cardinal of Brandenburg, the appearance of the dead body is softened by the supplicators and mourners and the same applies to Mantegna's representation (Brera, Milan). Holbein on the other hand depicts him as a body rigid in death, a study after nature done with scientific exactitude, and lacking all spiritual values, before which Dostojewski once exclaimed: 'This picture could rob many a man of his faith.' The dreadful sight is relieved only by the illumination of the features, which comes from below, and the shadows over the anguished eyes.

The same type and the lighting of a head from below recur in 'Joseph and the Shepherds' to the left on the left shutter of the Oberried altarpiece of 1520/21 (cf. Pl. 39). It cannot be ascertained whether the 'Dead Christ' belonged to this altar or to a lost work by Holbein, a 'Deposition', which has been preserved in an engraving by Wenzel Hollar, dated 1640 (*Parthey No. 109*), possibly reversed, and in a coloured drawing in the Louvre (*P. Ganz, C.R., C.15*). See Fig. 3.

In the Amerbach inventory we read 'ein todten bild H. Holbeins uf Holz mit olfarben (a dead man by H. Holbein, oil on wood) cum titulo Jesus Nazarenus Rex', whereas the inscription today has been increased by the word 'Judaeorum' and the individual words are separated by blue-winged angels carrying the instruments of the passion. In all probability the wooden frame and the inscription painted on several strips of parchment did not originate until the end of the sixteenth century.

16–17. INNER SIDES OF THE TWO SHUTTERS OF THE OBERRIED ALTAR-PIECE. 1520/21. Oil and tempera on fir wood. Each shutter $88\frac{3}{8} \times 43\frac{1}{4}$. *Freiburg i. Breisgau, University chapel of the Cathedral.*

PLATES 35–36 (37–44, 63)

16. THE BIRTH OF CHRIST AND THE ANNUNCIATION TO THE SHEPHERDS. Left shutter.   PLATE 35

A night scene with the infant Christ as the source of light, inspired by Hans Baldung's 'Nativity' of 1520 in

LANDSCAPE. DETAIL FROM PLATE 22

Fig. 3 (Cat. Nos. 15 and 17). Reconstruction

Munich. Holbein borrowed the motive of the boy's arms forming into wings from the same scene in Baldung's high-altarpiece in Freiburg, and also the 'Annunciation to the Shepherds in the background. An etching by Nicoletto da Modena of the 'Nativity', which was in the collection of the Basle printer Hans Amerbach, served as the prototype for the architecture.

17. THE ADORATION OF THE KINGS. Right shutter.
PLATE 36

In its general build-up this is also inspired by a work of Baldung, the 'Adoration' (Berlin Museum, No. 603 A), in which the second king is kneeling, the Moorish king dressed in white is standing next to him and a follower shading his eyes with his hands is looking up at the star of Bethlehem (Fig. 4); according to *W. Stein, Holbein,* the latter represents the artist himself. The dog is taken from Dürer's engraving of St. Eustace and the procession of the kings' followers approaching over the bridge at the rear is derived from a drawing by Holbein's father in the print-room in Basle. Holbein had already depicted the train of horsemen on the 'Crucifixion' of the eight passion scenes in a similar but less vivid manner; and he repeated it in the sketch for the town hall picture 'Sapor and Valerian' of 1521 (*Cat. No. 168*).

The left shutter with the infant Christ still wearing the

D

FIG. 4 (Cat. No. 17.) Detail from the 'Adoration of the Kings' (Plate 36)

bandage round his navel was executed before the pendant. The infant is the artist's first-born child, who on the right shutter is already able to sit in his mother's lap and appears to be a year older in the Solothurn altarpiece, dated 1522. Stylistically, too, the disposition on the right shutter is clearer, more strongly emphasized in its bearing on the main group and more effective spatially owing to the perspective treatment of the architecture.

The central panel appears to have been destroyed during the iconoclastic storms. If it was not a sculptured group—as I assumed for a reconstruction attempt of the altarpiece—but a painted panel which had to correspond in form to the shutters, then the scene must have been a 'Resurrection of Christ' or a 'Last Judgement', both of which unfold in several zones one above the other. Both compositions can be seen in Holbein's woodcuts, which show how he represented these scenes; the large woodcut with the 'Last Judgement' belongs to the print-room in Basle, a second version and a 'Resurrection' is contained in the 'Hortulus Animae' (*H. Koegler, Hans Holbein d.J., Die Bilder zum Gebetbuch, Basle 1943, p. 137–38 Pl. 20, 21*). Both scenes allow the problems of light already treated in the shutters to be further developed in the central panel and surpassed in the figure of Christ in Glory.

The 'Mourning over the Dead Christ', which I had formerly regarded as the sculptured central group, may have decorated the two outer sides of the shutters as a painting and in this manner and together with the 'Dead Christ' of the predella have formed a whole as suggested, always provided that they did belong to the contemporary Oberried altarpiece (Fig. 3). The donor of the altar, the councillor Hans Oberried (pl. 37 and 63), was born in Freiburg and settled at Basle as a merchant. After his marriage to Amelia Tschekkenburlin he entertained family relations with the wealthy merchant guild of Basle, which played a leading part in the State. In 1521 he was a member of the Council of Three which was in charge of building and also therefore of the painting of the large council room begun by Holbein in the same year. The two figure groups kneeling behind the arms of Oberried and Tschekkenburlin represent the donor and his family; to the left behind the donor, are three sons and three grandsons (the latter were added later), on the right three daughters and a daughter-in-law, Maria David, and his late wife, who had died in 1518. As some of the portraits of the children do not show the same quality as the portraits of the donors, it can be assumed that they, like the grandchildren, were painted by another hand or have been overpainted. The catalogue of the 1946 exhibition of paintings in the Freiburg Museum even suggests the collaboration of Hans Holbein the Elder and his assistants.

With the coming of the Reformation, Hans Oberried was expelled from office for, like Meyer, he was loyal to the old faith; he retired to Freiburg, where he died in 1543. The altarpiece, which probably stood in the 'Kleinbasler Carthause', where Oberried's uncle Tschekkenburlin was prior and one of his daughters lay buried, must have been destroyed during the iconoclastic storms; the shutters, which contained portraits, could be saved by the family and were brought to Freiburg, though they can only be ascertained there with certainty from 1554 on, when they were given their permanent place in the university chapel of the minster. There they still stand today and form the central panel of an altarpiece.

The donation was made by Elizabeth, the only one of Oberried's daughters to remain true to the old faith, and her second husband Anton Baer, on the occasion of the death of their uncle Dr. Ludwig Baer (cf. *P. Ganz, Weihnachtsdarstellung Hans Holbeins d.J., Die Flügel des Oberriedaltars in der Universitätskapelle des Münsters zu Freiburg im Breisgau*. Published by the Münsterbauverein in Freiburg i/Br. 1922).

18. BUST OF ST. SEBASTIAN. Fragment, about 1522. Oil and tempera on pinewood. $12\frac{1}{2} \times 9\frac{5}{8}$. *Stuttgart, Württembergische Staatsgalerie.*   FIGURE 5

The head, looking directly at the spectator, astonishes by its striking portrait character; this has led to the suggestion that it might be a self-portrait of the artist which he purposely idealized as he did the model for the

FIG. 5 (Cat. No. 18). ST. SEBASTIAN. Fragment

so-called Madonna of Solothurn. The old-fashioned fur cap is taken from Burgkmair's 'St. Sebastian' in the altarpiece with the emperor Constantine of 1505 (Nuremberg, Germanisches Museum). Cf. *P. Ganz, Eine unbekannte Heiligendarstellung aus Holbeins zweitem Basler Aufenthalt. Jahrbuch für Kunst und Kunstpflege in der Schweiz, vol. V, 1928/29, p. 305 ff.*

19–20. St. George with the Cross of St. George standing over the Dragon. St. Ursula in a royal Robe. Oil and tempera on pinewood. Inscribed and dated: Hans Holbein MDXXII (date renewed in part) $37\frac{1}{2} \times 16\frac{1}{2}$. *Karlsruhe, Staatliche Kunsthalle.* **Plates 45–46**

Judging by the curve of the bodies the two figures cannot have been pendants; but they can have formed the inner and outer panels of a shutter. St. Ursula is wearing the same amulet attached to the same chain as the young woman in the preliminary drawing for the 'Madonna of Solothurn' for whom his wife served as model. The over-emphasized contraposto in the figures, the old-fashioned haloes as well as the branches which stretch unorganically into the composition cannot be reconciled with Holbein's achievements in 1522. The paintings if they were meant as left side panel of the altarpiece (a possibility considered by *H. A. Schmid, Holbein, p. 178 ff.*), must either have originated earlier or else must be regarded as works of a collaborator.

Various writers, including *Davis* and *Christoffel*, have doubted their authenticity as works by Holbein the Younger; I myself in a lecture given in Solothurn in 1924 described them as studio works.

21. Altarpiece of John Gerster, Town Clerk of Basle. The so-called 'Solothurn Madonna'. Oil and tempera on wood. Signed and dated: H.H. 1522. $55\frac{1}{8} \times 39\frac{3}{8}$. *Solothurn, Kunstmuseum.* **Plate 47 (48–49)**

This Santa Conversazione, painted in the full spirit of the Italian Renaissance, is composed as an equilateral triangle which should be hung at a point slightly above eye level. The shape of the altarpiece and the rounded barrel vault supported by unadorned pillars suggest the possibility that the work may have fitted into a Romanesque wall of the old church of St. Ursus. The holy bishop on the right of the Virgin whose infula is embroidered with the portrait of St. Nicolas of Myra has been variously interpreted as bishop Martin of Tours and as St. Nicolas. In either case the representation of the saint with the beggar at his feet is rare. If, however, the panel was donated by the town clerk John Gerster at the end of the negotiations between Basle and Solothurn in 1522 for the Nicolas altarpiece, newly endowed in 1520, then it may rather be assumed that it is a St. Nicolas. The latter, in addition, was the patron saint of Nicolas of Diesbach, the bishop's vicar-general, who resided at Solothurn and was on friendly terms with Gerster. On one of the votive panels of the Weiss couple, which was painted in 1520 by Leonhard Beck, the pupil of Hans Holbein the Elder, St. Martin is represented as a

Fig. 6. (Cat. No. 21). Copy of the ' Solothurn Madonna'

bishop, at his feet an alms seeker (Augsburg, Maximiliansmuseum). The warrior on the left carrying the standard of the Theban legion is St. Ursus, the patron saint of the ancient house of God. A comparison with the child of the Oberried altarpiece shows that Holbein used little Phillip, his eldest son, as a model for the Christ Child and it can also be seen from a comparison with the study of the head in the Louvre (*Ganz, C.R. 5*) that his wife served as model for the Virgin; on the hem of the corsage are the words: 'Als in Ern' (always in honour). The two shields with the arms of Gerster and his wife Barbara Guldenknopf, which were woven into the carpet, replace the portraits of Hans Oberried and Jacob Meyer with their families as donors on their respective altarpieces. This restriction may indicate that conditions were imposed, particularly as Gerster appears also as a donor, by the prior's side, in an altar-panel of the 'Last Judgement', which he had donated earlier to the charterhouse of Kleinbasel.

The state of preservation, often described as poor, appears to show the original condition in some parts, for instance in the figure of St. Ursus, but the lining of the cloak hanging over Mary's right wrist shows a disfiguring overpainting; it is completely yellow, even on the sleeve, where it ought to be pink. A copy by Gregor Sickinger, in the Benedictine monastery of Einsiedeln, retains the original condition (Fig. 6). Holbein had used a similar group of three figures on his title page woodcut of the 'Civic Rights of Freiburg' of 1519; it suggests Italian prototypes, in particular Vincenzo Foppa's 'Virgin and Child' now in the Brera in Milan and Gaudenzio Ferrari's altarpiece in Pietra Rocca near Vasallo. The enamel-like smoothness of the colour and the colour

ANNA MEYER. DETAIL FROM PLATE 55

combinations, similar to the eight 'Passion' scenes, are the direct result of Lombard art and the Lombard technique of painting.

Between 1689 and 1717 the panel entered the chaplaincy *Allerheiligen ob Grenchen*, founded at that time, and there was recognized and purchased by Franz Zetter of Solothurn in 1864 and restored by Eigner in Augsburg.

In 1604 Hans Bock copied the child and by putting a serpent in his hand made him the conqueror of sin (Basle, *Öffentliche Kunstsammlung*). *H. A. Schmid* thinks that the frame was in the form of a gilded archivolte, which completed the architecture of the picture. I feel that the aforementioned suggestion fits in better with the coolness of the colouring (cf. *F. A. Zetter, Die Zettersche Madonna von Solothurn von Hans Holbein dem Jüngeren, p. 122 ff. in Denkschrift zur Eröffnung von Museum und Saalbau der Stadt Solothurn, 1902*).

22. NOLI ME TANGERE: CHRIST APPEARING TO MARY MAGDALEN. Composition of 1524–6, preserved in the present repetition dating from the second stay in England. Oil and tempera on oakwood. $30\frac{1}{4} \times 37\frac{1}{2}$. *Hampton Court, H.M. The King.*   PLATE 50 (51–54)

Stylistically the representation belongs to the altarpieces made during Holbein's second stay in Basle, more precisely after his return from France. The slender beauty and the costume of the graceful figure of Mary Magdalen recall the figures of the Virtues on the tomb of Michel Colombe in the cathedral of Nantes; the jar of ointment she is holding, too, is a piece of French majolica. Christ's gesture recurs in the title page of the Coverdale Bible of 1535 and in the woodcuts for Cranmer's catechism of 1548 (*Campbell Dodgson, Woodcuts designed by Hans Holbein for the English Printers, The Walpole Society's 27th vol., 1938/39*). Equally graceful female figures can be seen in the sketch 'Solomon and the Queen of Sheba' of 1537 (*Ganz C.R. 129*).

Opinions differ greatly as to the date of origin and authenticity of the painting. *Chamberlain* dates it 1520, *Bayersdorfer*, who first published it, about 1530; the first stay in England is assumed in *KdK*. and in recent times the second stay in England until about 1540 (*H. A. Schmid*). *Woltman* and *Davis* did not accept Hans Holbein as the author, *Christoffel* suspected a copy, but the work is without doubt genuine. It is mentioned as No. 33 in the posthumous inventory of Henry VIII in 1547. According to *E. Law, Holbein's Pictures at Windsor Castle, p. 32*, L. Sustris painted a similar picture (*C. Baker, Hampton Court Catalogue, 1929, p. 73*).

23. ALTARPIECE WITH THE MADONNA OF MERCY AND THE BASLE BURGOMASTER JACOB MEYER 'ZUM HASEN'. So-called Darmstadt Madonna. 1528/30. Oil and tempera on limewood. $56\frac{3}{4} \times 39\frac{3}{4}$. *Darmstadt, Grandducal Castle.*
PLATE 55 (56–57, 91–93)

In its natural conception of a devotional image and in its spiritualized beauty the painting, which was destined for a private chapel, marks the highest achievement amongst Holbein's religious subjects. It is true that reminiscences of Leonardo's 'Virgin of the Rocks' are to be found both in the structure and composition of the group and in the individual motives, but the direct borrowing from Italian art, which predominated in his early work after his return from Milan, has given way to a general assimilation into his personal style. During his stay in France, through the French Renaissance, Holbein absorbed once more, and this time more consciously than in Lombardy, the Italian style, at the same time intensifying his plastic feeling by studying French figural sculpture. The statuesque impression of the Virgin, the slight Gothic curve of the body and the attitude of mother and child can be seen in a similar form in the monumental statues of the Virgin by Michel Colombe and his school, as, for example, in the 'Vierge d'Olivet' in the Louvre, from the first quarter of the century.

The composition, built up with a sure sense of style, was rounded off by an architectural Renaissance frame corresponding to the spatial effect, variations of which can be seen in Holbein's late window designs; the richly differentiated colour modelling indicates an origin after the first stay in England during the years 1528/30. Already *His* maintained that 1526 was the earliest possible date because Anna, the Burgomaster's daughter, who was born in 1513, can scarcely be younger than 13; this may be true of the preliminary study (*Ganz, C.R. 16*), on which Anna is represented as a young girl with her hair hanging down her back; in the picture, however, her hair is done up and she wears a bridal wreath round it, which was added later to the original version, still visible in pentimenti. According to *Daniel Burckhardt*, a Basle girl was not allowed to wear this headdress—the so-called '*Jungfernbändel*' (maiden's hair-band)—until she was 16 and when she became engaged she was allowed to have it trimmed with fresh flowers; this custom, however, has not been traced back further than the seventeenth century (cf. *Daniel Burckhardt, Ein verschollenes Holbeinwerk in Zeitschrift für schweizerische Archäologie und Kunstgeschichte, vol. 9, 1947, part 2, p. 95 ff.*). The latest date of origin is 1530, because Anna's marriage must have taken place in that year, since of the ten children with which she presented her husband, Nicolas Irmy, five were born before 1536. Furthermore, Meyer may have died in 1530, as his wife is recorded as a widow in 1531. Since Meyer was the leader of the orthodox religious group in 1528, a particular significance attaches to his commissioning of the altarpiece.

Represented at the feet of the Virgin are Jacob Meyer 'zum Hasen' with his two sons, who are not mentioned in any records and whose death preceded his own, his two wives Magdalen Baer, who died in 1511, and Dorothea Kannengiesser, as well as Anna, his daughter from his second marriage. The face of the Virgin shows the ennobled features of Magdalena Offenburg. According to the recent discoveries of *Dr. Rudolf Riggenbach* (*Blätter aus der Walliser Geschichte, IX, vol. IV, 1943, p. 474*

E

ff.), the altarpiece in all probability adorned the small chapel of the Weiherhaus Gross-Gundeldingen, still standing today, which lay outside the city walls of Basle and had been bought by Meyer as early as 1508. It was not sold until shortly before his death. The panel became the property of Anna, the sole heiress, and her husband Nicolas Irmy, and through their daughter Rosina passed to the Burgomaster Remigius Faesch, whose second wife she was. The latter sold the picture to Lucas Iselin in 1606 for 100 gold crowns. The Amsterdam art dealer Le Blond bought it from the latter's heirs for 1000 Reichsgulden. In 1709 it was auctioned in Amsterdam together with the collection of Jacob Cromhout and fetched 2000 gulden. The catalogue describes it under No. 24 as follows: 'Een kapital stuk met twee Deuren (doors) verbeeldende Maria met Jesus op haer Arm, met verscheyde Knielende Beelden na 't Leeven (meaning an important work of the Virgin and Child and various kneeling figures) van Hans Holbeen.' (cf. *G. Hoet, Catalogus of Naamlyst van Schilderÿen, s'Gravenhage, 1752,* *1*, p. 133, No. 24). From a booklet 'Tour in Holland in the Year MDCCCXIX', the author of which has been identified (*Oud-Holland 1925*) as the Scottish collector and later general Sir John Murray (1768–1827), it appears that then the picture still belonged to an art dealer Croese in Amsterdam and only came to Paris after 1822, where it was purchased by Prince Wilhelm of Prussia. (This information I owe to Dr. Hans Schneider, Basle.)

The preliminary studies in chalk for Meyer, his second wife and his daughter are in the *Öffentliche Kunstsammlung* in Basle. An old copy in the picture gallery in Dresden is, according to *E. Major*, probably the work of Bartholomäus Sarburgh and in all probability was made for Marie de Medici, the wife of Louis XIII of France. From her collection it returned later to Amsterdam and thence to Venice. Until the second half of the nineteenth century this more colourful version was regarded as Holbein's original work and its dethronement in favour of the Darmstadt picture was preceded by a regular 'battle of the savants'.

II. PORTRAITS

24. Young man with a red Beret. Signed and dated: H. 1515. H. Oil and tempera on pine wood. $13\frac{3}{4} \times 11\frac{1}{2}$. *Darmstadt, Landesmuseum Hesse.*   Plate 58

The portrait belongs to the group from the Holbein workshop described above on p. 213 and attributed variously to the father (*Woltmann*), to Ambros (*His-Heusler*), and to Hans the Younger (*H. A. Schmid*). The inscription on the white band is old, but the first H has been renewed by a later, clumsy hand.

The preliminary studies for the portrait in the Kunstverein in Basle, formerly attributed to Ambros, were recognized by *H. A. Schmid* as the work of his brother Hans, an attribution supported by the left-handed stroke. On the other hand the difference between the painted portrait of 1515 and the double portrait of the burgomaster Jacob Meyer and his wife, which is dated 1516, is so great, both in the spiritual conception of the model, in the colouring and in the technique of the execution, that in my opinion there can be no question of the same author. *Baldass* attributes the work to Hans Holbein the Elder, emphasizing as characteristic for his art the rich modelling, the thinness of the paint and the pale brilliance of the colours and also the sensitive rendering of the expression (*Baldass, Niederländische Bildgedanken im Werke des älteren Hans Holbein. Augsburger Kunst der Spätgotik und Renaissance, p. 158 ff.*). Both scholars attribute the preliminary drawing and the portrait to the same artist although the expression and pose of the person portrayed are not the same. There is, in my opinion, only one solution that will satisfy the complicated problems of stylistic criticism involved: we must assume that the drawing is by Hans and the painting by his brother Ambros; the delicate and light colours point rather to the latter than to Hans.

25–26. Double Portrait of the Burgomaster of Basle Jacob Meyer and his Wife Dorothea Kannengiesser. Signed and dated: H.H. 1516. Oil and tempera on limewood. Each picture $15\frac{1}{8} \times 12\frac{1}{4}$. *Basle, Öffentliche Kunstsammlung.*   Plates 59–60

The two portraits were joined to form a diptych, the front of which was adorned with the Meyer arms (Fig. 7). Later corrections and changes can be seen on both paintings. According to *Stoedtner*, composition and conception are influenced by Hans Burgkmair's clairobscur woodcut portrait of Johannes Baumgartner of 1512.

The preliminary silverpoint and red chalk drawing (*Ganz, C.R., 1 and 2*) came to the *Öffentliche Kunstsammlung* from the Faesch Museum together with the double portrait.

Jacob Meyer 'zum Hasen' (1482–1531) was a moneylender by profession, which is indicated by the coin in his left hand. He took part in the Italian campaigns, fought at Marignano and in 1516 was elected the first bourgeois mayor. This unusual honour seems to have been the pretext for the portrait. As early as 1521 he was

FIG. 7 (Cat. No. 25). ARMS OF THE BURGOMASTER JACOB MEYER

removed from office and punished for accepting a foreign pension, but thanks to his wealth and position as leader of the orthodox group of citizens he retained an influential standing (see *Cat. No. 23*).

Dorothea Kannengiesser (about 1490–1549), Jacob Meyer's second wife, was the daughter of a Habsburg tax collector from Thann in Alsace; he married her in 1513, two years after the death of his first wife Magdalena Baer.

27. JUNKER BENEDICT VON HERTENSTEIN (about 1495–1522). Inscribed and dated: DA · ICH · HET · DIE · GESTALT · WAS · ICH · 22 · JAR · ALT · 1517 · H. H. PINGEBAT. (When I looked like this, I was twenty-two years old, 1517, H.H. painted it.) Tempera on paper, recently transferred to wood. 20¾ × 15½. *New York, Metropolitan Museum*.   PLATE 61

Benedict von Hertenstein, the eldest son of the Lucerne magistrate Jacob and his second wife Anna Mangold, became a member of the Great Council in 1517 and was killed in 1522 at the battle of Bicocca. Holbein also portrayed him on horseback and at the feet of St. Benedict on two wall paintings inside the Hertenstein House, wearing the same riding jacket and with the same gold chain inherited from his mother. The triumphal procession on the wall frieze is a free interpretation of a prototype by Mantegna, which was available in an engraving, from which Holbein also borrowed the procession on the house façade.

Through the mediation of the Basle painter Wocher, the portrait passed into the collection of Daniel Burckhardt-Wild in Basle, whose heirs sold it to England in 1819. The Earl of Cork and Orrery sold it through Christie's in 1905, and in 1906 it was bought by the Metropolitan Museum. Its authenticity has not remained unchallenged. *Roger Fry* (*Burlington Magazine, X, 1906, p. 48 f.*) thought it was possibly by Ambros Holbein, and *Christoffel* (*p. 60*) does not consider it genuine.

28. ELDERLY MAN WITH A CAP OF PLAITED GOLD BRAID, probably the Lucerne magistrate Jacob von Hertenstein. Traces of the date 151(7) and monogram. Oil and tempera on wood. 18½ × 14½. *London, art dealer*.
                                                                      FIGURE 8

My attempt to identify the man portrayed with Holbein's patron Jacob von Hertenstein (*Burlington Magazine XXXVIII, May, 1921, p. 210 ff.*) is based on the fact that the same person on the copy of one of the wall paintings in the Hertenstein House in Lucerne can be identified as the master of the house who, in company with his son Benedict, his wife and suite is out duck shooting. In addition the same figural motives on the architectural frame recur on Holbein's design for the façade of the house. The painting in Lucerne, which a later inscription describes as a portrait of Jacob von Hertenstein (*Bericht der Gottfried Keller Stiftung 1932–1945, p. 96*), has no connection with Holbein and represents a different person.

The old-fashioned composition, a synthesis of various borrowed motives, is in striking contrast to the incisive character and lively treatment of the head, which recalls the Meyer portrait of 1516. My attribution to Holbein the Younger (see above) has been contested by *Ernst Buchner*; he claims it as a work of the elder Hans, for whom he thinks the disposition as a whole more characteristic (*Ernst Buchner, Zum Werk Hans Holbeins des Älteren, Beiträge zur Geschichte der deutschen Kunst, Augsburg 1928, vol. II, p. 156 ff.*). Today I am largely in agreement with this view but am still convinced that Hans the Younger collaborated on the head. *Stein* suggested Sigmund Holbein as the author. The picture, which was discovered in 1928, belonged to the Winn/Ellis collection in London.

29. TWO SKULLS IN A WINDOW NICHE. About 1517. Brown monochrome. Oil and tempera on limewood. 13⅛ × 10⅛. *Basle, Öffentliche Kunstsammlung (Amerbach-Kabinett)*.   FIGURE 9

The picture described in the Amerbach inventory D (1586) as 'Ein klein hültzin täfelin doruf zwen todtenkopf mit gefelschten farben' (a small panel with two skulls with false colours) is today attributed to Ambros Holbein. It may have formed the outer sides of the double portrait of the two boys joined together as a diptych which the preliminary studies and the style definitely show to be a work of Ambros (*Öffentliche Kunstsammlung*). But the artistic quality and the intensely vivid, realistic rendering are more in keeping

FIG. 8 (Cat. No. 28). SUPPOSED PORTRAIT OF JACOB VON HERTENSTEIN

FIG. 9 (Cat. No. 29). Outer side of diptych

with the spirit and ability of Hans Holbein and for that reason I regard it as a work that must be attributed to him though it shows once again the close collaboration of the workshop.

30. THE BASLE JURISPRUDENT BONIFACIUS AMERBACH (1495–1562). Signed and dated: IO · HOLBEIN · DEPINGE-BAT · M · D · XIX · A · PRID · EID · OCTOBR. Oil and tempera on pinewood. 11¼ × 10⅞. *Basle, Öffentliche Kunstsammlung (Amerbach-Kabinett).*   PLATE 62

The man portrayed was the youngest son of the book printer and publisher Johannes Amerbach, a native of Swabia; Bonifacius studied law under Zasius at Freiburg and under Alciat at Avignon and in 1525 became professor of Roman Law at Basle university. Erasmus, for whom the picture was probably painted, was so intimate with him that he made him his sole heir. During the iconoclastic storms Amerbach rescued several of Holbein's works and in so doing laid the foundation for the famous art collection which was systematically built up by his son (cf. *Paul Ganz, Die Amerbach als Kunstsammler, Jahresbericht der Amerbach-gesellschaft, 1920*).

The Latin distich on the writing tablet, for which a whole page of rough drafts in Amerbach's writing has been preserved (*vol. D IV, p. 407*), runs in English: 'Though only in paint, I do not deviate from life and my true lines give a noble portrait of my master. Fine art has

formed him in me just as nature let him develop after eight times three years of his life.'

31. ELDERLY MAN WITH BLACK CLOTH CAP. The date 1520 was on a later inscription. Oil and tempera on nut wood. 7⅞ × 6¼. *New York Art Market (1938).*   FIGURE 10

The yellow inscription removed during the restoration, which had probably been transferred to the back when the original frame was replaced, reads: A · XX · M(ensis) SEPTEMB · XVIII · E(tatis) · L VIIII · M(ensis) · VII · D(iis) · X · III. The man portrayed must have been a citizen of Basle who belonged to the circle of Holbein's patrons. According to the investigations of *Dr. August Burckhardt* he could have been the councillor Eucharius Holzach, magistrate of Kleinbasle and justiciary of Grosshueningen who died in 1521. In any case it is the type of bourgeois portrait customary for that period and is closely related stylistically to the one of Hans Oberried (Plate 37) on the altarpiece of 1521.

The picture appeared on the Paris art market in 1927 (cf. *P. Ganz, Ein unbekanntes Bildnis aus Holbeins Baslerzeit in Jahrbuch für Kunst und Kunstpflege in der Schweiz, 1924/27, part I, p. 173 ff.*).

32. YOUNG MAN WITH A BLACK BERET. 1520. Oil and tempera on oak. 7⅞ × 5⅞. *London, Private Collection.*

FIGURE 11

The small-sized picture is an example of a simple bourgeois portrait which, in spite of its poor state of preservation, can lay claim to be an original. Preliminary drawings have been preserved for similar portraits (cf. *P. Ganz, C.R. 3.* Engraved by Wenzel Hollar dated MLXX; ibid., 4 and 465.).

33. THE BASLE PRINTER JOHANNES FROBEN (1460–1527). About 1522/23. Oil and tempera on oak. Inscribed on the parapet: IOANNES · FROBENIVS · TYP · HHOLBEIN · P. 19¼ × 12¾. Enlarged in Charles I's time as pendant to an Erasmus portrait. *Hampton Court, H.M. The King.*
FIGURE 12

Johannes Froben, born at Hammelsburg in Franconia, became a citizen of Basle in 1490. He was the publisher of Erasmus' books and his fatherly friend, with whom the scholar stayed when in Basle.

The picture, which has had an architectural frame painted in later in the manner of Steenwyck, was published by *Lionel Cust*, after the overpainting had been removed, as a genuine work by Holbein (*Apollo 1927, vol. V, No. 30, p. 249*). In the catalogue of the exhibition of the King's Pictures, London 1946/47, this picture and its pendant are attributed to an early imitator of Holbein. Nevertheless after the removal of the additions the portrait of Frobenius does seem to reproduce the Holbein original from which the copy in the Basle museum (*KdK. 208*) was made, omitting the parapet.

It is not improbable that Froben commissioned the first portrait of Erasmus as a pendant to his own which would explain why Erasmus, in spite of his importance, had to be shown turned to the left, on the right-hand side, which from the sitters' position is the left and according

FIG. 11 (Cat. No. 32). YOUNG MAN WITH BLACK BERET

FIG. 10 (Cat. No. 31). ELDERLY MAN WITH BLACK CLOTH CAP

to the custom of the time the less important. In any case it can be stated with certainty that at the beginning of the seventeenth century a double panel with portraits of the author and his publisher was still in the possession of the Faesch family in Basle and was then purchased by the art dealer Le Blond, sold to the Duke of Buckingham and given by the latter to Charles I. It is described in the *Humanae Industriae Monumenta* of *Remigius Faesch* as two panels attached by iron hinges that can be opened and closed; in addition Faesch notes that he had the two paintings, sold by his father in 1648, copied by the Basle painter Joh. Sixtus Ringlin when he heard that they were to be auctioned in London.

The double panel at Hampton Court might be a copy of the original made in Amsterdam, which Le Blond had overpainted and passed on to London. He also had the Madonna of the Burgomaster Jacob Meyer '*zum Hasen*', that he owned, copied.

34. ERASMUS OF ROTTERDAM (1467-1536) STANDING BEHIND A TABLE. Inscribed and dated: IOHANNES HOLBEIN · MDXXIII. Oil and tempera on wood. 30 × 20⅛. A strip added along the bottom and along the side. *Longford Castle, Earl of Radnor.* PLATE 64

In one of the marginal drawings for the 'Praise of Folly' in Basilius Amerbach's copy, Holbein had already represented the famous scholar sitting at his desk (*Ganz, C.R., L.64*), at a time when he was still unacquainted with the latter's habits. When Erasmus came to live with his publisher Froben in Basle in 1522, Holbein was able to study him more thoroughly and always painted him standing, as was his custom, behind his writing desk. The date appears on the cover of the book in the book-stand leaning against the bottle. The distich with Holbein's name on the leaves along the edge was certainly composed by Erasmus and reads:

(IL) LE EGO IOANNES HOLBEIN NON FACILE (VLL) VS
(TAM) MICHI (MIMVS) ERIT QVAM MICHI (MOMVS ERA)T.

The wine bottle may be a reminder of the delicate scholar's preference for heavy Burgundy wines as a tonic for his weak digestion. The Greek inscription on the book cover on which he has placed his hands, *ΗΡΑΚΛΕΙΟΙ ΠΟΝΟΙ* (The Labours of Hercules), and that along the vertical side '*ERASMI ROTERO(DAMI)*', allude to Erasmus's idea that 'unkindly fates had burdened him with an Herculean task' (*Huizinga, Erasmus, p. 161*). As we know from a letter he wrote to Pirkheimer on June 3, 1524, this painting is one of the two portraits he sent to England. One was destined for the Archbishop of Canterbury, who was portrayed by Holbein three years later in the same position standing behind a table. The preliminary drawings for the two hands in black and red chalks (*Ganz, C.R. 6, 7*) are in the Louvre.

In 1616 this portrait was in the possession of the Earl of Arundel, who had probably bought it from the London collector de Loo. In 1655 it belonged to the Howards in Albury; it was purchased by Viscount Folkestone at the auction of Dr. Mead's collection together with the portrait of Petrus Aegidius by Quentin Metsys, which had at one time belonged to More.

An excellent replica, from the same time as the original a little softer and more colourful in its general effect, belonged to Walter Gay in Paris (*KdK. 206*).

35. ERASMUS OF ROTTERDAM WRITING. 1523. Oil and tempera on paper mounted on pinewood. 14⅛ × 12. *Basle, Öffentliche Kunstsammlung (Amerbach-Kabinett).* PLATE 65

An anonymous woodcut of Upper German origin (illustrated in *Emil Major, Erasmus von Rotterdam, Basle 1926, T.4*) gives a portrait of the writing man in profile with the date 1522, whereas the year of the Basle picture is fixed by the text that Erasmus is writing on the paper in front of him, the beginning of his Commentary of the Gospel of St. Mark written in 1523. It runs: 'In evangelium Mar(ci) paraphras(is) per/Erasmum Roterodamum autor(em) cunctis mortalibu(s) ius/item est.' A contemporary copy giving the head the same size, as a roundel, against a light blue ground bears the words: Anno 1523. The same portrait figure in front of a large, flowered damask curtain was copied as a woodcut by Hans Rudolf Manuel in 1550 from an original, which at that time belonged to Amerbach, for Sebastian Münster's Cosmography. This portrait, which has since been lost, was possibly done in 1522.

The portrait in the Basle museum is damaged, the present green background is suspect and the hands are overpainted; but carriage and countenance of the sitter show the clear beauty of the master's art. *Solomon Vögelin* suggests that this portrait is the one that Erasmus sent with Holbein in the spring of 1524 as a present to Bonifacius Amerbach, who was studying at Avignon. *H. A. Schmid* considers the picture to be a workshop production painted over by Holbein, *Christoffel* an original painted over by another hand.

36. ERASMUS OF ROTTERDAM WRITING. After 1523. Oil and tempera on pinewood. 16⅞ × 13. *Paris, Louvre.* PLATE 66

The painting, which was probably intended as a present for an English patron, has the same motive as the small portrait in Basle. But it reveals a deeper, more intellectual conception in the slight inclination of the head and in the plastic modelling of the face as well as in the richer and more picturesque setting with the dark, colourful oriental carpet hanging on the panelled wall. A study in black chalk of the writing hand is on the same sheet as the preliminary drawing for the left hand of the portrait at Longford Castle (*Ganz, C.R., 7*).

On the back of the picture is an inscription written on a scrap of paper: 'This picture of Erasmus Rotterdamus was given to the Prince by Adam Newton' and the seal of the Newtons. Under the guidance of Lord Arundel, Prince Henry, eldest son of James I, became an enthusi-

FIG. 12 (Cat. No. 33). THE BASLE PRINTER JOHANNES FROBEN
Reproduced by gracious permission of H.M. The King

astic art collector. Through him the picture came into the possession of Charles I, whose collector's mark is branded twice on the back; later it was given to King Louis XIII of France in exchange for Leonardo da Vinci's 'St. John the Baptist'.

37. SELF-PORTRAIT WITH A RED BERET. 1523/24. Black and coloured chalks on white paper, cut out along the outlines. 16⅛ × 13½. *Basle, Öffentliche Kunstsammlung (Amerbach-Kabinett).* PLATE 67

The portrait mentioned in the Amerbach inventory in 1586 as a 'conterfehung Holbein's mit trocken farben' (portrait of Holbein in dry colours), was never questioned until 1892, when the identification was challenged by *Berthold Haendke* on the basis of a not very convincing anatomical comparison with the self-portrait in Florence. *Dr. Andreas Werthmann,* professor of pathology at Basle University, convincingly refuted this proof and maintained that the two drawings in Basle and Florence represent the same person (*Identifizierung des Basler Selbstbildnisses Holbeins d. J. in Jahrbuch für Kunst und Kunstpflege in der Schweiz, 1929/30*). Nevertheless *Haendke's* opinion has been adhered to by a number of writers, for instance *H. A. Schmid* (*Anzeiger für Schweizerische Altertumskunde 1931, p. 280 ff.*) and *Georg Schmidt* (*Jahresberichte der Öffentlichen Kunstsammlung, Basle, 1943, p. 144 ff.*).

The portrait, formerly square-shaped, was cut down at the sides during a restoration and cut along the contours and coloured with watercolours; the face and hair were altered and gone over with coloured chalk. Seeing that Holbein tried the coloured chalk technique for the first time in 1523 ('Head of a Leper', *Ganz, C.R. 8*) but only mastered it fully in France, the portrait may date from 1523/24, when he was 26 or 27 years old (cf. *P. Ganz, Das Bildnis Hans Holbeins d. J. in Jahrbuch für Kunst und Kunstpflege in der Schweiz 1929/30, and C.R. 11*).

38. PORTRAIT OF A WOMAN, PROBABLY THE ARTIST'S WIFE. 1523/24. Oil and tempera on oak. 17¾ × 13⅜. *The Hague, Mauritshuis.* PLATE 68

In pose and position of the hands, the portrait, which was at one time attributed to Leonardo, recalls the Mona Lisa that Holbein could have seen first in Milan, where it was copied by various artists and later, the original, in France. From the collection of Charles I it passed to the Earl of Arundel, where it is described in the catalogue of 1655 as 'ritratto della moglie di Holbein'.

The similarity of the features to those of the preliminary study for the Madonna of Solothurn and to the woman on the family portrait in Basle of 1528/29 is increased by the dull eyes looking out beneath heavy eyelids, so-called 'dropsy' eyes, which the family portrait depicts in an advanced stage of the disease. As in the portraits of Magdalena Offenburg (*Cat. No. 39–40*), the free and charming attitude can be traced to French influence.

Holbein's authorship is not universally accepted: *Davies* rejects the picture and *H. A. Schmid* regards it as a good, old copy of an original executed in 1516. The use of oak is also suspect, as this material is not known to have been used during the artist's second stay in Basle; on the other hand the artistic quality is Holbein's own and I reproduce it here even if, as I myself formerly assumed, it is a copy of a vanished original (*KdK., note 50*). The picture, which bears the Collector's Mark of Charles I, passed from the Arundel Collection to that of Joan de Vries, Mayor of Amsterdam (Sale 13 October, 1738) and G. van Slingeland, before it was acquired by William V of Orange.

39. MAGDALENA OFFENBURG AS VENUS. 1526. Oil and tempera on limewood. 13⅝ × 10⅞. *Basle, Öffentliche Kunstsammlung (Amerbach-Kabinett).* PLATE 69

The woman portrayed, a daughter of the wholesale merchant Bernhard Tschekkenburlin and widow of Hans Offenburg (died 1518), a son of the Basle mayor Peter, lived with two daughters who, like herself, led a loose life. It is just conceivable that Magdalena had her portrait painted in the French manner, like Diane de Poitiers, as a goddess; but it is quite certain that she did not commission her portrait as Laïs of Corinth (*Catalogue No. 40*). The two portraits, mentioned together in the Amerbach inventory of 1586 as 'zwei täfelin doruf ein Offenburgin conterfehet ist' (two panels with likenesses of Magdalena Offenburg) are nevertheless, as symbols for true love and mercenary love, pendants and belong together; they may have been painted for a wealthy lover. It is possible that this picture, too, once had an inscription, which was cut out later, as *H. A. Schmid* assumes; there is no mention of it in the inventory. *His-Heusler* regarded the Cupid as Holbein's son Philipp.

40. MAGDALENA OFFENBURG AS LAÏS CORINTHIACA. Inscribed and dated: LAIS : CORINTHIACA : 1526. Oil and tempera on limewood. 13⅝ × 10⅝. *Basle, Öffentliche Kunstsammlung (Amerbach-Kabinett).* PLATE 70

The restrained pose and charming gesture of the Swiss lady, represented as a Greek hetaera, reveal, like the Venus, the influence of French portrait painting, which is also apparent in the colouring and in the more flowing manner of the painting. *Woermann* was the first to point out that the outstretched right hand is copied from Christ's left hand in Leonardo da Vinci's 'Last Supper' in the refectory of S. Maria delle Grazie in Milan.

Holbein twice used Magdalena Offenburg as a model for his series of women's costumes (*Ganz, C.R., 146, 149*) and also for the Virgin on the altarpiece of the burgomaster Meyer, where she can be recognized by her slender build and lovely, oval-shaped face.

41. SIR THOMAS MORE (1477/78–1535). Dated: M · D XXVII. Oil and tempera on wood. 29¼ × 23¼. *New York, Frick Collection.* PLATE 71 (72–74)

Thomas More, the son of Sir John More, lawyer and judge, studied at Oxford, first philosophy and theology and later jurisprudence; in 1494 he entered New Inn as a lawyer, and Lincoln's Inn in 1496. He was a Member of

Parliament in 1504, King's Councillor in 1518, knighted in 1521, Speaker of the House of Commons in 1523 and Lord Chancellor of England in 1529, succeeding Cardinal Wolsey. He resigned office in 1532 after refusing to take the oath on the new law of succession to the throne; later he was accused of high treason and executed in 1535.

More, whose friendship with Erasmus of Rotterdam went back to his student days, wrote 'Utopia' as a pendant to Erasmus' 'Praise of Folly'. It was published first in Latin and then in German by Frobenius in Basle with woodcuts from drawings by Ambros Holbein. He was Holbein's first patron in England. Two preliminary drawings for More's portrait still exist; the study, which was probably done as early as 1526 (*Ganz, C.R. 18*), corresponds exactly to the sketch for the family picture, the second one, on the other hand, is the model for the portrait dated 1527 (*Ganz, C.R. 25*). Both drawings are at Windsor Castle (cf. *K. T. Parker, The Drawings of Hans Holbein in the Collection of H.M. the King at Windsor Castle, 1945, Nos. 2 and 3*).

According to *Chamberlain* (*vol. 1, p. 304*) a portrait of Thomas More belonged to Lord Lumley in 1590 and in 1785 it was sold from Lumley Castle to Mr. Hay in London; another belonged to the Duke of Orleans in 1727, whose pictures were auctioned in London in 1786. The one in the Frick Collection was formerly the property of Mr. Edward Huth in Dublin.

Rubens copied the portrait during his stay in England 1629/30 (Prado No. 1688); a miniature is in the Pierpont Morgan Collection in New York. Many copies of the portrait exist in various sizes.

42. ALICE MIDDLETON, LADY MORE. 1527. Oil and tempera on oak. $14\frac{1}{2} \times 10\frac{5}{8}$. *Corsham Court near Bath, Lord Methuen.*   PLATE 76

Alice Middleton was More's second wife; this small portrait is a coloured study for the large family picture, for which the corresponding coloured chalk study is missing (cf. *P. Ganz, Zwei Werke Hans Holbeins d. J. aus der Frühzeit des ersten englischen Aufenthaltes in Festschrift zur Eröffnung des Basler Kunstmuseums, 1936*). A miniature with the portrait of 'Alicia, wife of Sir Thomas More' was in the 'Portrait Miniature Exhibition' of 1865 at the South Kensington Museum, No. 1146 (Collection J. Heywood Hawkins).

43. LADY WITH A SQUIRREL AND A MAGPIE. About 1528. Oil and tempera on oak. $21\frac{1}{4} \times 15\frac{1}{4}$. *Houghton Hall, Norfolk, Marquess of Cholmondeley.*   PLATE 75

The person portrayed wears the same fur cap as Margaret Giggs, the adopted daughter of Thomas More, on the preliminary drawing for the family portrait (*Ganz, C.R. 29; Parker, W.Dr. 8*); in any case she belonged to the More circle.

The presence of the squirrel, which at that time, like the magpie, was a popular domestic animal, recalls Leonardo's 'Girl with an Ermine' in Cracow; the many pentimenti indicate that Holbein painted the portrait from nature; this also explains the spontaneous expression and the vivid effect of the finely modelled flesh tones.

The portrait was discovered in 1925 in Cholmondeley Castle, Malpas, Cheshire (cf. *P. Ganz, An unknown portrait by Hans Holbein the Younger, Burlington Magazine, XLVII, Sept. 1925*).

44. SIR HENRY GUILDFORD (1478/79-1532). Inscribed and dated: Anno D. MCCCCCXXVII / Etatis Suae xlix. Oil and tempera on wood. $32\frac{1}{8} \times 26$. *Windsor Castle, H.M. The King.*   PLATE 77 (79)

Guildford holds the wand of office as 'Comptroller of the King's Household' and wears the collar of the Garter, which was given to him for his services at the siege of the fortress of Thérouanne in 1527. This honour was the pretext for the commissioning of the portrait. A preliminary drawing is also at Windsor Castle (*Ganz, C.R. 20; Parker, W.Dr. 10*).

The portrait was formerly at Lumley Castle and later in the Arundel Collection; in 1732 it was found by Vertue in London and probably purchased by Queen Caroline (cf. *P. Ganz, Zwei Werke Hans Holbeins d. J. aus der Frühzeit des ersten englischen Aufenthaltes in Festschrift zur Eröffnung des Basler Kunstmuseums, 1936*).

For the companion portrait see the following note.

45. MARY WOTTON LADY GUILDFORD. Pendant. Inscribed and dated: ANNO M D XXVII ÆTATIS SVÆ XXVII. Oil and tempera on wood. $31\frac{1}{2} \times 25\frac{5}{8}$. *St. Louis, U.S.A., Fine Art Museum.*   PLATE 78 (80)

The lady represented was the second wife of Sir Henry Guildford; she outlived him and later married Sir Gawin Carew, brother-in-law of Charles Brandon, Duke of Suffolk. She was small, whereas her husband was a giant. Holbein sought to counterbalance this in the double portrait by adding the columns.

A preliminary drawing, seen in a rather more frontal view, is in the *Öffentliche Kunstsammlung* in Basle (*Ganz, C.R. 21*).

In 1590 both the portrait and the pendant were at Lumley Castle; the former being entered in the catalogue of the collection as an original work by Holbein; both portraits came into the possession of the Earl of Arundel, who had them engraved in 1647 by Hollar. Another version belonged to the Duke of Buckingham at Stowe. The painting, which had long been forgotten, came to light at an auction at Sotheby's in London on 13th May 1930 as 'Flemish School, Portrait of Dame Elizabeth Bullen' and fetched £15,500. Aquired by the St. Louis Museum in 1943.

A smaller copy, formerly belonging to W. K. Vanderbilt, is in the Metropolitan Museum in New York and also a miniature (*Catalogue of Early English Portraiture, London, 1909, Plate XXXII, Case D. 3*).

46. William Warham, Archbishop of Canterbury (1456/57–1532). 1527. Inscribed and dated: Anno Dm M D xxvij Etatis sue lxx. Oil and tempera on wood. 30 × 25¾. *London, Lambeth Palace.* PLATE 81

Before becoming Bishop of London and shortly after Archbishop, Warham had been ambassador in Rome, Flanders, Burgundy and at the Court of the Emperor. In this capacity he became Chancellor of the University of Oxford and, still under Henry VII, Lord Chancellor of England. He was a friend and patron of Erasmus.

The life-sized preliminary study for the head of the aged Archbishop is at Windsor Castle; it is executed in black and coloured chalks on white paper and in spite of its poor state of preservation is extraordinarily vigorous and characteristic (*Ganz, C.R., 19; Parker, W.Dr. 12*). A second drawing of the same size and on the same paper, also by Holbein, is on the London art market.

Of the two painted portraits the smaller one at Lambeth is more spontaneous and more incisive in the drawing as well as more uniform in the colour effect. During the civil war it was stolen together with a portrait of Erasmus but later was bought privately and returned to Lambeth Palace (*Wornum, 1867, p. 218*).

47. William Warham, Archbishop of Canterbury (1456/57–1532). 1527. Inscribed and dated: Anno Dm M D xxvij Etatis sue lxx. Oil and tempera on wood. 32⅛ × 26⅜. *Paris, Louvre.* PLATE 82 (83–84)

This portrait, which was originally larger and was recently cleaned, must be classified as an original replica of the portrait at Lambeth Palace. Warham had it painted in return for the portrait of Erasmus that he had received in 1524. Holbein painted the Archbishop in the same pose as Erasmus. This replica is less precise in the drawing and modelling but richer and rather softer in the colour effect; the execution shows the same meticulous care. The yellow-brown damask curtain has been replaced by a green one but the folds have been retained and in addition further slight colour changes can be seen in the dress and in the accessories.

This version belonged to the Newton family, who owned several works by Holbein, and from them it passed into the collection of Andries de Loo in London. Later it was purchased, probably with all the Holbeins belonging to de Loo, by the Earl of Arundel and at the latter's auction was bought for the collection of King Louis XIV. An excellent copy hangs today in the National Portrait Gallery in London.

48. Nicolas Kratzer (1487–1550), Astronomer of King Henry VIII. Dated: 1528. Oil and tempera on wood. 32⅝ × 26⅜. *Paris, Louvre.*

PLATE 85

On the table of the scholar, who is represented at work, is a sheet of paper with a three-line Latin inscription: Imago ad vivam effigiem expressa Nicolai Kratzeri monacenssis q(ui) bavarus erat quadragessimū (primū) annu tpre (tempore) illo (com)plebat 1528.

Kratzer, who was born at Munich, entered Henry VIII's service early after studying at Corpus Christi College, Oxford, and working as a teacher. He belonged to Thomas More's circle and taught the latter's daughters astronomy.

The Louvre version, formerly in the Arundel Collection, came into the possession of Louis XIV after the auction of that collection. It is not, however, the portrait that Carel van Mander saw in the collection of Andries de Loo in 1604 as has been previously supposed. This second version was bought by Sir Walter Cope, the builder of Holland House, and belonged to his heirs for more than 300 years. It shows the completed original composition as does the portrait in the Louvre since its recent cleaning. Of other copies a miniature in the Pierpont Morgan Collection may be mentioned.

49. Thomas Godsalve (1481–1542) **and his Son John** (about 1510–1556). Dated: Anno Dni MDXXVIII. Oil and tempera on oak. 13¾ × 14¼. *Dresden, Staatliche Gemäldegalerie.* PLATE 86

The Godsalve family came from Norfolk, where the father was a notary and court registrar at Norwich; he is writing his name and his age on the sheet of paper in front of him: Thomas Godsalve de Norwico Etatis sue Anno quadragesimo septo. The son later entered the service of the court and had his own and his wife's portrait painted by Holbein (*Catalogue No. 91–92*).

The portrait was in the Arundel Collection and later in Paris, where it was purchased in 1749 for the Elector of Saxony.

50. Sir Henry Wyatt of Allington Castle (died 1537). 1527/28. Oil and tempera on oak. 15⅜ × 12¼. *Paris, Louvre.* PLATE 87

Sir Henry Wyatt was already in the service of Henry VII and in 1509, on the accession of Henry VIII, was made a member of the Privy Council. He belonged to Thomas More's circle. His son, the court poet Thomas Wyatt, was also portrayed by Holbein. The picture has disappeared but a preliminary drawing is at Windsor Castle (*Ganz, C.R. 88; Parker, W.Dr. 64*).

The authenticity of the portrait, which has been distorted by heavy overpainting, is not universally accepted; according to *W. Waetzoldt (Hans Holbein der Jüngere, Berlin 1939)* the free, bold conception is not characteristic for Holbein.

The painting formed part of the Arundel Collection and was sold by Viscount Stafford, the earl's son, to the Cologne collector Jabach, from whom it was bought by the French minister Colbert for Louis XIV's collection. Several copies exist, among them one of the same size in the National Gallery of Ireland; the head alone is in the former Spiridon Collection in Rome.

51. SIR BRYAN TUKE (born about 1470). 1528 or 1532/3. Inscribed BRIANVS TVKE, MILES, ANᵒ ETATIS SVÆ LVII / DROIT ET AVANT. Oil and tempera on oak. 19¼ × 15⅝. *Washington, National Gallery (Mellon Collection).*

PLATE 88

The age of the sitter being unknown, it is only possible to date the picture on stylistic grounds. The strong emphasis on the physical mass of the body and the expression still dependent on the outline drawing suggest the last year of the first stay in England; the gold lettering at the side of the head, however, points to the early years after Holbein's return to London when, as early as 1532, he was using lines of text with the age and date as effective horizontal accents in the composition of his portraits. The motto is authentic but the writing on top seems to be a later addition; it may possibly be a repetition of an inscription that was formerly on the frame. In any case it does not fit in with the composition nor was it Holbein's custom to use commas instead of full stops. The unperspective two-line proverb written on the cover of the book bottom left: NVNQVID NON PAVCITAS DIERVM MEORVM FINIETVR BREVI? (from Job, Vulgate, X, 20) is not by Holbein but has been added later.

In 1509 Bryan Tuke became Clerk of the Signet, later secretary to Cardinal Wolsey, and in 1528 Treasurer of the Royal Household and French secretary to the king. Like Sir Thomas Wyatt he belonged to More's circle.

The example reproduced here was formerly the property of the Methuens of Corsham Court; it was purchased in 1848 at the Sanderson auction by the Marquess of Westminster and later sold by his heirs. *Lionel Cust* dated the portrait 1539/41 (*Burlington Magazine, vol. XVII, p. 193 ff.*), which is accepted as 'probably correct' by *H. A. Schmid* in *Thieme-Becker, Künstlerlexikon.*

A second version, also of good quality, which in 1678 belonged to Lord l'Isle (cf. *J. R. Haig Evelyn's Diary*), passed from the Hugh Blake collection, London, to the U.S.A. and with the collection of Francis F. Prentiss to the Cleveland Museum of Fine Art (cf. *R. R. Tatlock* in *the Burlington Magazine, XLII, p. 246*).

The third version in the Alte Pinakothek in Munich is regarded today as a workshop copy; it is mentioned as early as 1590 in an inventory of the works of art of the House of Wittelsbach but without the later addition of Death with an Hour Glass approaching the figure from behind the green curtain (repr. *in KdK. 211, see note p. 251, and K. Voll, in Süddeutsche Monatshefte 1905, p. 177*).

52. THE ARTIST'S FAMILY. Dated: 152(8/9). Oil and tempera on a sheet made up of four pieces of paper cut out along the outlines of the figures and mounted on wood: 31¼ × 25¾. *Basle, Öffentliche Kunstsammlung (Amerbach-Kabinett).*

PLATE 89 (90)

Holbein's wife Elizabeth Binzenstock was the widow of a Basle tanner, Ulrich Schmidt called Schliffstein, and owned a modest fortune. The two children are Philipp,

born in 1521, who later learnt the goldsmith's trade in Paris and returned to Augsburg, and Katharina, who afterwards married the butcher Jacob Gyssler of Basle.

The group, described in the Amerbach inventory in its present condition, is cut down on the right side; the girl's fingertips are missing which can be seen on various copies, and also the last digit of the date. One copy (*KdK. 212*), on which the group is represented in a Renaissance interior, may possibly give an indication of the original condition; another in the Lille museum shows the group in front of a blue background with an inscription in two lines above it (*KdK. 213*).

The painting appears to have been sold during Mrs. Holbein's lifetime, for a record in a Zurich legal document shows that in 1542 it belonged to the portrait painter Hans Asper, who was much influenced by Holbein and was probably his pupil (cf. *Diethelm Fretz, Hans Asper, der Besitzer des Holbeinschen Familienbildes* in *Anzeiger für schweizerische Altertumskunde, 1923 p. 205 ff.*). He used it as a model for the portrait he painted in 1549 of Regula Gwalter, the daughter of Zwingli, and her little daughter Anna (Zurich, Central Library). It was of such value to him that he refused all offers to buy it. And so the work, which had already been discovered by Amerbach's agent, the painter Jacob Clauser, could only be purchased after Asper's death in April 1579 through the good offices of the apothecary Georg Clauser at a price of 6 Kronen (*P. Ganz and E. Major, Die Entstehung des Amerbachschen Kunst-Kabinetts und die Amerbachschen Inventare, Basle 1907*).

53. PHILIP MELANCHTHON (1497–1560). 1529/30. Oil and tempera, portrait on the bottom, and ornament with inscription on the lid of the original wooden box. Diam. of box 4¾, of the picture 3½. *Landesmuseum, Hanover.*

PLATES 94–95

Philip Schwarzert, called Melanchthon, was appointed schoolmaster at Tübingen in 1514 and professor at Wittenberg in 1518; in 1530 he published the Latin version of the Augsburg Confession and after Luther's death he became the 'Praeceptor Germaniae'.

Holbein may have met Melanchthon at Erasmus in Freiburg when Melanchthon visited his mother in Bretten; in any case the ornamental work framing the inscription on the cover allows us to date the portrait from the third stay in Basle. This inscription on the cover reads: QVI CERNIS TANTVM NON, VIVA MELANTHONIS ORA, HOLBINVS RARA DEXTERITATE DEDIT (If you were to see Melanchthon's face you would not see as much as through Holbein's skill). The picture comes from the Royal Hanoverian Collection and was formerly in the royal palace at Georgengarten (*Catalogue Molthan, 1844, p. 66, No. 14*). The grey monochrome decorations framing the inscription on the cover are not repeated in a replica which came to Montreal from the Horace Walpole Collection; the inscription is transferred to the frame (Sir William van Horne Collection).

SQUIRREL. DETAIL FROM PLATE 79

54. THE PRINTER JOHANNES FROBEN OF BASLE (1460–1527). 1528/32. Oil and tempera on oak. 4¼ diam. *Maidenhead Thicket, Sir Thomas Merton.* PLATE 96

There can be no doubt that the roundel was painted after the half-length portrait (*Catalogue No. 33*) during Holbein's third stay in Basle. It was probably commissioned by Frobenius' son, the godchild of Erasmus, presumably as a pendant to the roundel of Erasmus painted at that time. A stencilled reproduction was made in 1671 by A Blooteling (*Wurzbach, Niederländisches Künstlerlexikon, I, p. 120, No. 16*). It was formerly in the collection of M. G. Pretyman of Orwell Park and was auctioned at Christie's in 1934.

55–60. ERASMUS PORTRAITS.

A second group of portraits of the scholar was painted by Holbein after his return to Basle from England. With the exception of the small roundel they required no further studies from nature. They show Erasmus in the same position and with his head in three-quarter profile to the left, similar to the portrait of 1523 at Longford Castle. He is either standing behind a table with his hands on a closed or open book or without the table with his hands folded across his chest. Both groups show variations which may be Holbein's own.

Of the three versions of the first group, one (Leningrad) is an exact replica of the 1523 figure but reduces the rich interior to a mere indication of a corner of the room and a cast shadow on the wall; the second dated 1530 (Parma) shows the scholar before a blue background with his left hand resting on an open book, which he is holding with his right hand, whereas on the third version (Turin) both hands are placed on the book lying on the table in front of him. The variations in the second group are slight, the scholar is either represented behind a parapet, which conceals his hands (Paris, Zurich) or free with his hands more or less in evidence (New York).

The roundel in Basle, which was probably preceded by a fresh meeting between the artist and Erasmus, who had been living at Freiburg-im-Breisgau since April 1529, must have originated 1531/32; it is confined to a portrait bust without hands; the attitude remains the same but the strongly illuminated features of the old man surpass all previous portraits in the spiritualized power of the expression. It is the masterpiece of the whole group. This painting, too, was copied many times: one copy belongs to the gallery at Karlsruhe; another, in the Lanckoronski collection in Vienna, has the signature of Georg Pencz and the date 1532 (cf. *P. Ganz, Les portraits d'Erasme de Rotterdam in Revue de l'art ancien et moderne, 1932* and *Die Erasmusbilder von H. Holbein d. J. in Gedenkschrift zum 400. Todestage des Erasmus von Rotterdam, Basle 1936, p. 260 ff.*)

55. ERASMUS OF ROTTERDAM, half-length portrait, standing behind a table. Dated: 1530. Oil and tempera on wood. 13 × 10. *Parma, Gallery.* FIGURE 13

As stated above this picture was painted from studies or from a painting of 1522/23. The picture in question may

FIG. 13 (Cat. No. 55). ERASMUS OF ROTTERDAM. 1530. Parma, Gallery

be the one sent by Professor Conrad Goelenius of Löwen to Johannes Dantiscus, Bishop of Kulm. Goelenius had it specially painted after the bishop had refused the offer of an older version belonging to him (*Chamberlain*). The picture was etched by Van Dyck.

A very similar one (regarded as genuine by *Woltmann*) is at Turin, of which, like the one at Parma, many copies exist.

56. ERASMUS OF ROTTERDAM STANDING BEHIND A PARAPET. About 1530/1. Oil and tempera on wood. 7 × 5⅛. *Paris, Collection Baron Maurice de Rothschild.* FIGURE 14

The painting was at one time in Spain, where it had been brought from Flanders by the Marquis de Moncade (*Catalogue de l'Exposition de l'Art suisse à Paris, Jeu de Paume, 1924*).

Another version is in a private collection in Zurich; it comes from the collection of the sculptor Hildebrandt in Munich and is illustrated in original size in *H. A. Schmid, Hans Holbein d. J., Basle 1945, fig. 61.*

57. ERASMUS OF ROTTERDAM. 1530/31. Oil and tempera on wood. 7⅜ × 5¾. *New York, Pierpont Morgan* (formerly). FIGURE 15

The small piece of paper on the wall with an illegible text, which distinguishes this version from all the others,

F

FIG. 15 (Cat. No. 57). ERASMUS OF ROTTERDAM
New York, Pierpont Morgan

FIG. 14 (Cat. No. 56). ERASMUS OF ROTTERDAM
Paris, Maurice de Rothschild

Fig. 17 (Cat. No. 59). ERASMUS OF ROTTERDAM
Private Collection in U.S.A.

Fig. 16 (Cat. No. 58). ERASMUS OF ROTTERDAM
New York, Wildenstein Galleries

was not painted in until the seventeenth century, for it does not occur on an engraving by Lucas Vorsterman made from this version.

On the reverse side a piece of paper from Henry VIII's time is stuck on with the words: Haunce Holbein me fecit, Johanne(s) Noryce me dedit, Edwardus Banyster me possedit. The two men named were well-known personalities at the English court (cf. *Sidney Colvin* in *Burlington Magazine Nov. 1907*). Later the picture came into the Arundel Collection and then belonged to the Howards of Graystoke; it was purchased from them in 1907 by Pierpont Morgan.

58. ERASMUS OF ROTTERDAM 1530/31. Oil and tempera on limewood. $7\frac{1}{4} \times 5\frac{5}{8}$. *New York, Wildenstein & Co.*

FIGURE 16

The portrait, which was owned by the kings of Saxony, is already mentioned in the oldest inventory of the Kunstkammer Saxony and may have been a present from Erasmus himself to the Elector of Saxony. A copy by Joerg Pencz, dated 1537, is at Windsor Castle.

59. ERASMUS OF ROTTERDAM. 1530/31. Oil and tempera on pinewood. $7 \times 5\frac{3}{4}$. *U.S.A. Unknown Private Collection.*

FIGURE 17

The execution of this version is as masterly as that of No. 58; the position of the hands is varied slightly, similar to No. 57. It was formerly in the Brockhaus Collection in Leipzig.

60. ERASMUS OF ROTTERDAM. 1531/32. Oil and tempera on the bottom of a boxwood case. Diam. 4. *Basle, Öffentliche Kunstsammlung (Amerbach-Kabinett).*   PLATE 97

Holbein may have painted the little roundel on the occasion of a visit to Erasmus at Freiburg; it is not possible to establish with certainty whether it was intended for Hieronymus Froben, the godson of the scholar, as a pendant to the portrait of his dead father, which he had copied by Holbein, or whether it was part of the inheritance of Bonifacius Amerbach. Holbein drew a similar portrait of Erasmus, with the portrait of Luther as a pendant, for the 1533 edition of the 'Adagiorum opus' of Erasmus. Copies of the roundel are at Karlsruhe, Cassel and elsewhere. (Cf. *H. Koegler, Zum graphischen Werk der Brüder Holbein, Jahresbericht der Öffentlichen Kunstsammlung Basel, 1919–20.*)

61. THE HANSEATIC MERCHANT GEORG GISZE OF DANZIG. (1497–1562). Dated: Anno dom. 1532. Oil and tempera on oak. $37\frac{5}{8} \times 33\frac{3}{4}$. *Berlin, Deutsches Museum.*

PLATE 98 (99)

The merchant, represented in life-size, is standing in a quiet attitude behind his desk in his sensibly furnished office. He is opening a letter the address of which reads: Dem erszamen Jergen Gisze to Lunden in engelant Mynem broder to handen (to my brother George Gisze in London). The name occurs also as Gyse and Gisse in the documents of the Steelyard and is identical with that of the patrician Cologne family Gueiss, many members of which were in the Hanseatic colony in London (*Chamberlain*).

According to the catalogue of the Berlin Museum, Georg Gisze belonged to a branch of the Cologne family which had settled in Danzig; his brother Thadman, canon and at that time Bishop of Danzig, had received a brevet from King Sigmund of Poland, on which were the same arms as those on the signet ring lying on the table. The trademark on the seal and on the letter has also been traced to the Danzig Giszes.

The description of the milieu, carried out down to the minutest detail, which appears here for the first time, gives a personal atmosphere to the room and in no way spoils the unity of figure and spatial composition in spite of the superb rendering of each individual object; it heightens one's interest in the person, shows his love of beautiful things and gives information as to his character and mode of living.

On the table, which is covered with a costly Oriental carpet, are not only all the objects required for letter writing and a pair of scissors, but also a lovely glass vase with a bunch of carnations, a reminder of Gisze's engagement, a clock and a metal box with some coins. A piece of paper has been stuck with sealing wax to the top left side of the panelled wall on which a Latin distich is written: Διονχιòν [sic] i Imagine Georgii Gysenii: Ista refert vultus, quā cernis, imago Georgi / Sic oculos vivos, sic habet ille genas / Anno aetatis suae XXXiiij / Anno dom̄. 1532 (The picture that you see here records the features of Georg / such are his lively eyes, such is his face). At the left, the sitter's motto and name appear on the wall in cursive letters: Nulla sine merore voluptas— G. Gisze (No joy without sorrow). On the wall to the right are various other papers, one of which bears the address: Dem Erssame vorsichtige Jerge Gysse to Lund in Engelant (fig. 18-19),

This beautifully executed work seems to have been a trial piece in which Holbein wished to reveal his skill; it really did bring him in a number of commissions from the Hanseatic merchants.

The picture was auctioned in London in 1785 with the Duke of Orleans' gallery and was purchased by Christian von Mechel, who offered it in vain to the Basle University authorities. In 1821 it entered the Solly Collection and passed with this collection to the Berlin gallery (cf. *P. Ganz, Aus dem Geschenkbuch der Öffentlichen Kunstsammlung in Basel* in *Jahresbericht der Öffentlichen Kunstsammlung in Basel, 1913, p. 30/31*).

62. A HANSEATIC MERCHANT BELONGING TO THE LONDON STEELYARD, the so-called Goldsmith Hans of Antwerp. Dated and inscribed: Anno dni 1532 auf 26 (?) Julij / Aetatis suae.... Oil and tempera on wood. $25 \times 18\frac{3}{4}$. *Windsor Castle, H.M. The King.*   PLATE 100

The identification with the goldsmith Hans of Antwerp is based on the address of the letter which he is holding in his hand and is about to open, as well as on Holbein's

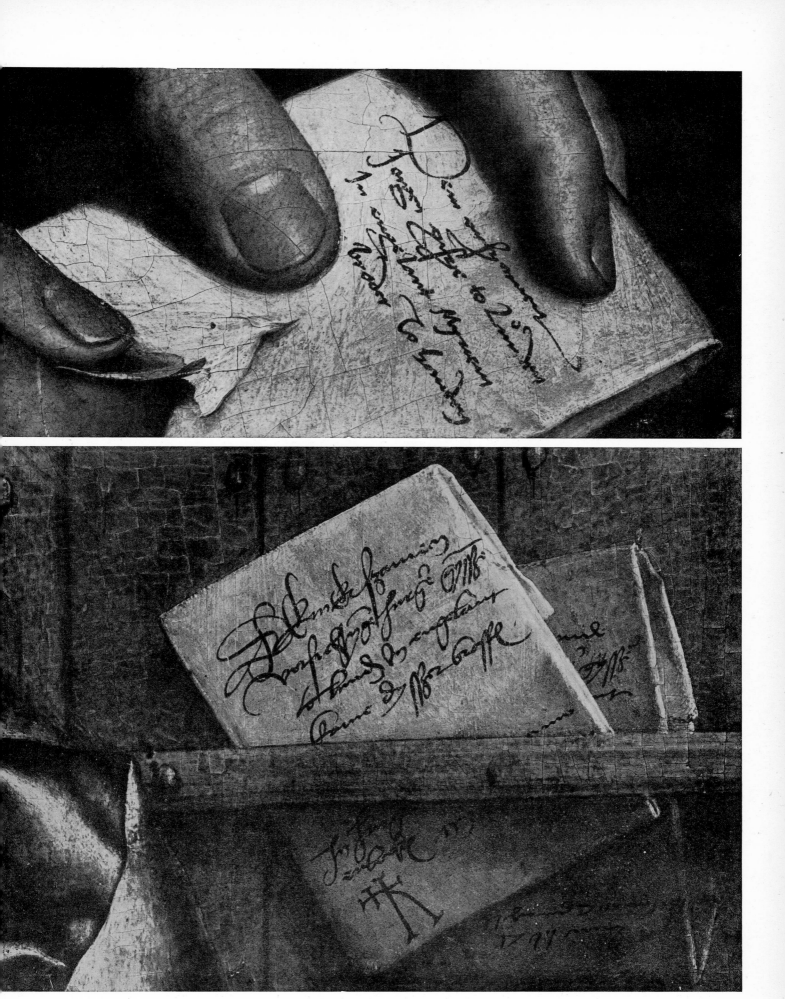

FIGS. 18-19 (Cat. No. 61). Details with inscriptions from the portrait of George Gisze (Plate 98)

relationship to Hans of Antwerp, for whom he worked and who was one of the witnesses of the artist's will. The inscription which is nearly destroyed, reads: 'Dem ersamen — (a) . . . An . we . p . . . Stallhof to L . . .' The seal, however, engraved with a W and the coins on the table seem to indicate a merchant rather than a goldsmith. The picture formerly belonged to the collections of the Duke of Buckingham, Charles I and James II; it was sold under the Commonwealth for £100 (*Chamberlain*).

63. THE SO-CALLED GOLDSMITH HANS OF ANTWERP.
Inscribed: ETATIS SVÆ 35. About 1533. Oil and tempera on oak. Diam. 5⅛. *London, Victoria and Albert Museum (Salting Bequest).* PLATE 101

The man portrayed here front face is without doubt the same person as the one on the two three-quarter-face portraits at Windsor Castle and Blankenburg (*Catalogue No. 62 and 64*). He wears a ring on the first finger of his left hand as he does on the portrait of 1532. The indication of the age enables us to determine the missing figure on the portrait of 1532, for the roundel cannot have originated much later than 1532/33.

If these portraits, of which the smaller one in half-profile was regarded from the beginning of the seventeenth century as a self-portrait of Holbein, do represent Hans of Antwerp, the latter must have been born in 1497/98, a contemporary of Holbein. It is certain that the artist was on intimate terms with a man he portrayed three times. This was the case with Hans of Antwerp, for Holbein made many designs for goldsmith's work for him, including a drinking cup with his name (*Ganz, C.R. 206*). Published for the first time in the catalogue of the exhibition 'Early English Portraiture' in the *Burlington Fine Arts Club 1909. p. 129.*

64. THE SO-CALLED GOLDSMITH HANS OF ANTWERP.
After 1533. Oil and tempera on pinewood. Diam. 4⅛. *Schloss Blankenburg, Duke Ernest August of Braunschweig-Lüneburg.* PLATE 102

The third portrait, in which Holbein shows the head in three-quarter view looking to the left, has slight variations in the hair and the beard and a firmer, more intellectual expression. It must be of later origin than the other two, though on the reverse side is written in Dutch: J. Holbein a. 1532 out (old) 34, thus giving the age (34) missing on the portrait at Windsor Castle.

It is probably one of the two versions seen by Carel van Mander in Amsterdam in 1604; it was engraved before 1612 by A. Stock and published by H. Hondius as a self-portrait of Holbein.

The painting was in the Royal Collection at Hanover and has often been reproduced; an excellent replica is in the collection of the Earl of Spencer at Althorp (cf. *KdK. 226*).

65. THE MERCHANT HERMANN WEDIGH OF COLOGNE
(1503–1560). Inscribed: H.H. on the book-cover and dated: ANNO . 1532 . ÆTATIS SVÆ. 29. Oil and tempera on wood. 15¾ × 12¼. *New York, Metropolitan Museum.* PLATE 103

On the signet ring of the sitter are the arms of the patrician family Wedigh of Cologne; he has been identified by *Wilhelm Geelen* as Hermann Wedigh III, who after his stay at the London Steelyard became councillor in Cologne and judge in Niederich.

The device 'Veritas odium parit' (Terence, *Andria*, v. 22) appears on the paper in the book. The initial letters of the owner, HER WID, are painted as an ornament along the edge of the leaves (cf. *Beiträge zur Kölnischen Geschichte, Sprache und Eigenart, II, parts 10 and 11, Jan. 1917. W. Geelen, Mitteilungen über Porträts des Kölner Patriziergeschlechts von Wedigh*).

This portrait and the second Wedigh portrait were formerly in the Schönborn gallery in Vienna. It was first recognized as a portrait of a member of the Cologne family Wedigh by *Theodor von Frimmel* (*Kunstchronik XXII, 1887, p. 379*); later it was more accurately designated as 'probably Hermann Wedigh' (*Kleine Gemäldestudien II, part III, 1896, p. 41 ff.*). *Bode* described the sitter as a member of the Trelawney family (1887). *Reber and Bayersdorfer* published the portrait in 'Klassischer Bilderschatz' 1889, No. 94, as a self-portrait of Holbein aged 29.

Through Duveen the picture came into the Stout Collection in Chicago; later it belonged to Edward S. Harkness, New York, and after the latter's death passed to the Metropolitan Museum.

66. THE MERCHANT HERMANN HILLEBRANDT WEDIGH
OF COLOGNE. Inscribed and dated: ANNO 1533 ÆTATIS SVÆ 39. Oil and tempera on oak. 15⅜ × 12. *Berlin, Deutsches Museum.* PLATE 104

In this portrait, too, the man described as 39 years of age was identified by the arms on his signet ring. It is not possible, however, to establish his identity exactly; he may have been a brother or a cousin of Hermann III.

The picture formerly belonged to the Count of Schönborn in Vienna and came to Berlin with the Suermondt Collection in Aachen.

67. THE MERCHANT DIRK TYBIS OF DUISBURG.
Dated: March 1533. Oil and tempera on wood. 19 × 13⅞. *Vienna, Kunsthistorisches Museum.* PLATE 105

The address on the letter he is holding in his hand, which is from his brother, reads: Dem ersamen Derek Tybys van Dusborch alwyl Toe Dard / off wae hy yss myn lyffen broder f. In front of him are two other documents, a seal with the trademark and the initials D.T., a pen and knife and a round metal box containing inks and money, as on Gisze's portrait. On the paper on the left is written: †Jesus† Da ick was 33 jar alt was ick Deryck Tybis to London / dyser gestalt en hab dyser gelicken den mael gesch (rieben) / myt myner eigener hant en was halffs mert anno 1533/per my Deryck Tybis fan Dus. . . .

The trademark has been drawn between the Christian name and the surname (*Baldass, Catalogue of the Vienna Museum, 1928*). The Tybis were domiciled in Duisburg and Cologne.

In 1781 the portrait was at Schloss Belvedere in Vienna.

68. THE HANSEATIC MERCHANT CYRIACUS KALE. Inscribed and dated: IN ALS GEDOLTIG SIS ALTERS 32/ANNO 1533. Oil and tempera on wood. 23⅝ × 17⅛. *Brunswick, Herzog-Anton-Ulrich Museum.*   PLATE 106

In addition to his correspondence the elegant, soberly dressed merchant holds a pair of leather gloves in his left hand. Judging from the dialect of the device which Holbein painted on the dark blue background as pendant to the inscribed age, Cyriacus Kale was of Upper German origin. The addresses on the two letters identify him. They read: Dem ersamen syriacuss Kalen to Luden up stalhoff sy disser briff, and: Dem Ersamen f(esten) syriacus Kallenn in Lunde . . . stalhoff sy dies(er) . . . . The overpainting has been removed from the light flesh tones, which, like the hands, reveal the grey underpainting.

69. THE MERCHANT DERICH (Dietrich) BORN OF COLOGNE (1510–1549). Inscribed and dated: DER BORN ETATIS SVÆ · 23 ANNO 1533. Oil and tempera on wood. 23¾ × 17¾. *Windsor Castle, H.M. The King.*   PLATE 107

The sitter was also one of the merchants of the steelyard in London. He had a second, smaller portrait painted of himself which bears the same age indication. The scrolls in the background are fig leaves; a distich is on the parapet carved into the stone:

DERICHVS SI VOCEM ADDAS IPSISSIMVS HIC SIT /

HVNC DVBITES PICTOR FECERIT AN GENITOR

(Add but the voice and you have his whole self, that you may doubt whether the painter or the father has made him).

Former Collections: King Charles I, Earl of Arundel, King Charles II.

70. THE MERCHANT DERICH BORN OF COLOGNE. Inscribed and dated: DE(R) BOR(N) / (AE)TATIS SVÆ (23) MDXXX (III). Tempera on paper mounted on wood, cut at both ends. 3½ × 2¾ (originally round, diam. 3½). *Munich, Alte Pinakothek.*   PLATE 117

As opposed to the large, representative portrait, this small one, originally in the form of a roundel, gives only the head of the young Hanseatic merchant, with sides reversed. It may originally have been a study. The picture was formerly in the gallery at Mannheim.

71. JOHN or WILLIAM RESKIMER OF MURTHYR. 1532/3. Oil and tempera on wood. 17½ × 12½. *Windsor Castle, H.M. The King.* (Formerly at Hampton Court.) PLATE 108

The identification as John Reskimer, assumed until now, is not certain but what is certain is that the portrait represents one of the sons of the wealthy, landed nobleman William Reskimer Murthyr, whose country seat was in Cornwall. In 1527 John was in the King's service and in 1535 High Sheriff of Cornwall. William, the younger brother, entered the king's service as a page in 1532.

The preliminary drawing for the portrait is in the Royal Collection at Windsor Castle (*Ganz, C.R. 75; Parker, W.Dr. 31*).

The painting was given as a present to Charles I and is also mentioned in the inventory of Charles II.

72. ROBERT CHESEMAN OF DORMANSWELL, the so-called Falconer of Henry VIII. Inscribed and dated: ROBERTVS CHESEMAN · ETATES SVÆ · XLVIII / ANNO D M M D XXXIII. Oil and tempera on wood. 23¼ × 24⅝. *The Hague, Mauritshuis.*   PLATE 109 (110)

Robert Cheseman of Dormanswell, whose father Edward was Justice of the Peace for Middlesex in 1528, came from a long, distinguished line of landed gentry. According to *Chamberlain*, he cannot have been one of the falconers in the service of Henry VIII as these were minor court officials and with their salary of 20s. to 25s. a month could never have afforded to commission portraits.

The picture, formerly in the collection of the English Royal Family, was taken to Holland by William III of Orange; after his death Queen Anne in vain demanded its return. An old copy was exhibited in 1890 at the Tudor exhibition in London (173 A).

73. SIR NICOLAS CAREW, MASTER OF THE HORSE OF HENRY VIII (about 1490–1539) On the paper, bottom left, probably painted in later, is written: Sr Nicholas Carewe Master of the Horse to King Henry y 8. Oil and tempera on wood. 35⅞ × 40. *Drumlanrig Castle, Scotland, Duke of Buccleuch.*   PLATE 111 (112)

The preliminary drawing for the head in black and red chalks is in the *Öffentliche Kunstsammlung* in Basle; it certainly belongs to the period of the first stay in England, and is probably from the same time as the studies for the portrait of Henry Guildford and his first wife: later Holbein no longer drew on untinted white paper (*Ganz, C.R. 33*). Stylistic criteria however, suggest, that the portrait must have been completed after Holbein's return to England, 1532/3, as it shows a ceremonial conception which he developed at that time.

In 1524 Carew succeeded his brother-in-law Guildford as equerry to the king, whom he also served as ambassador and general. In 1536 he was invested with the Order of the Garter but in 1537 he fell into disgrace and ended on the scaffold in 1539.

Until 1842 the portrait was in the house built by Carew at Beddington; a copy at Lumley Castle was sold in 1785.

74. THE FRENCH AMBASSADORS AT THE ENGLISH COURT: JEAN DE DINTEVILLE (1504–1557) AND GEORGES DE SELVE (1509–1542). Inscribed and dated: JOANNES / HOLBEIN / PINGEBAT / 1533. Oil and tempera on wood. 81½ × 82½. *London, National Gallery.* PLATE 113 (114–116)

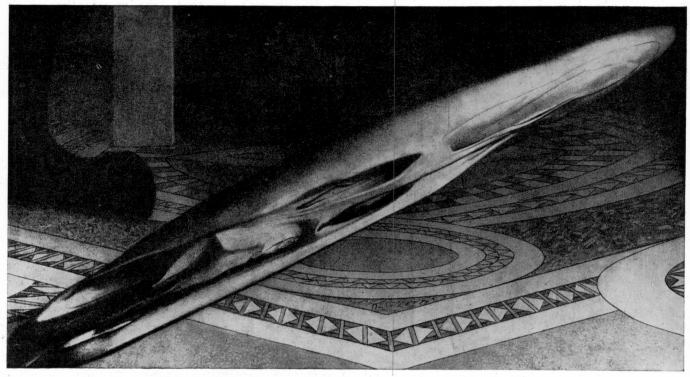

FIG. 20 (Cat. No. 74). DISTORTED SKULL. Detail from the 'Ambassadors' (Plate 113)

FIG. 21 (Cat. No. 74).
Photographic correction of the distorted skull

STILL LIFE. DETAIL FROM PLATE 113

The person on the left, a knight of the Order of St. Michael, is Jean de Dinteville, seigneur de Polisy, who was five times ambassador of King Francis I in London. His age is inscribed on the scabbard: AET · SVE 29. the name of his family seat is on the globe.

The figure on the right in a violet soutane is Georges de Selve, Bishop of Lavour, a great scholar and music lover, who thirteen years later represented France at the Diet of Spires. His age is inscribed AETATIS SVÆ 24 along the edge of his bible. Georges de Selve spoke German fluently and was one of the few people occupying a high position among the French clergy who harboured sympathy for the Reformation and hoped for and advocated an understanding between the catholic and protestant doctrines and the Church. This attitude is indicated by the open hymn book with, on the left side, the opening lines of Luther's choral song 'komm heiliger Geyst + Herregott, erfüll mit Deiner gnaden gut deiner gläubigen hertz, mut und sinn', and on the right the first lines of the song 'Mensch willtu leben seliglich und bei Gott bliben ewiglich / sollt du halten die zehen Gebot die uns gebent unser Gott'. Both hymns are in the little book of hymns by Johann Walter published in Wittenberg in 1524. The small book on the left shows a page of the *Merchant's Arithmetic* by Petrus Apianus published in 1527 at Ingolstadt.

The instruments on the two shelves of the table, which is covered by an Oriental carpet, indicate the interest in the free arts eagerly fostered by the two men. The mosaic pattern of the floor was copied by Holbein from the *Opus Alexandrinum* which still covers the floor of the sanctuary at Westminster Abbey and was constructed at the beginning of the fourteenth century under Abbot Richard Ware by Italian workmen. The silver crucifix in the left corner above Dinteville's head, half concealed by the green curtain, must also, like all the other objects, have a symbolic meaning; it may be connected with the strange object in the foreground, the distorted human skull, which only becomes apparent in its true, foreshortened form to a spectator approaching from the left. I am indebted to Mr. E. Th. Goppelsroeder-Sarasin, Basle, for the photographic correction (Fig. 20–21). As Dinteville also has the skull on his cap badge, *Miss Mary Hervey's* assumption that this 'Memento mori' was his personal device gains in probability.

The identification of the two men and the explanation of the objects crowded into the picture have been given by *Miss Mary F. S. Hervey* in her book *Holbein's Ambassadors, the Picture and the Men*, London, 1900. She reverted to the old French tradition of the 'Ambassadors', which in England had been supplanted by the identification with two Englishmen, the court poet Thomas Wyatt and his friend, the antiquary John Leland. *Woltmann* and *Wornum* accepted this explanation without question; later the attempt was made to identify the two men with the Dukes Otto Heinrich and Philipp the Valiant of Pfalz-Neuburg. The picture was taken to France by Dinteville. On the marriage of his niece Claude, it passed with the castle of Polisy, where it was, to François de Cazillac, baron

of Assac (1562), whose heirs after the sale of Polisy took it with them to the Château Milhars in Languedoc and later to their town house in Paris. In 1787 it can be identified at the Beaujon auction and in 1790 belonged to the art dealer Jean Baptiste Pierre Lebrun, the husband of the paintress Vigée-Lebrun. After it had been engraved by J. O. Pierron, Lebrun sold it to England, There it was purchased by the second Earl of Radnor, one of whose successors, the fifth earl, sold it from Longford Castle to the National Gallery for £55,000.

75. GEORGE NEVILL LORD ABERGAVENNY (1460/61–1535). 1533/34. Oil and tempera on oak. $15\frac{1}{8} \times 12$. *New York, Mrs. A. W. Erickson.*   FIGURE 22

George Nevill, third earl of Abergavenny, general and statesman in the service of Henry VIII, was invested with the Order of the Garter in 1513; the badge with the George is visible beneath the fur-lined coat.

The preliminary drawing for this picture is in the collection of the Earl of Pembroke at Wilton House (*Ganz, C.R. 37*).

The portrait painted from it exists in many versions, two of which bear the inscription:AETATIS LXXIIII, but dated: A° MDXXXIIII and AN 1533. A miniature in the collection of the Duke of Buccleuch (Plate 189, *Catalogue No. 133*) is a replica of the bust of the same painting.

The version illustrated here is the best known today;

FIG. 22 (Cat. No. 75). LORD ABERGAVENNY

although it is by no means preserved in its original condition it does show Holbein's art both in the general conception and in the details. It was formerly at Boughton-Malherbe in Kent, the seat of the Earl of Stanhope, whose family had inherited it from Thomas Lord Wotton.

76. Sir Henry Guildford (1478–1532). 1532/33. A repetition by the artist of his portrait of 1527. Oil and tempera on oak. 4½ diam. *Detroit, Institute of Arts.*

PLATE 119

The small portrait was the bottom of one of the wooden boxes in vogue at that time, which usually had two subjects, one on the bottom and one on the lid. The portraits painted as pendants of a court official of Henry VIII and his wife in the Vienna gallery are one such example. Possibly Guildford's wife commissioned a box of this kind after the death of her husband; an etching by Wenzel Hollar of 1647 (*P. 1410*), which gives her bust in the round, after the painting of 1527, lends support to such a theory.

The modellihg of the face in grey colour with the lights heightened in white formed the underpainting, after the manner of a wash drawing, on which the colour of the face was glazed (cf. *Detroit Institute of Arts, Catalogue of Paintings, 1944, p. 62*).

77. Bust of a young Man with a Carnation. Dated: ANNO 1533. Oil and tempera on wood. 4⅞ diam. *Banbury, Estate of Lord Bearsted.* PLATE 118

The painting was sometimes regarded as a self-portrait of Holbein; the man is probably a German merchant of the Steelyard.

The portrait, which *Zahn* had regarded as genuine but heavily damaged, was formerly in the collection of Jäger, Gsell and Pržibram in Vienna and also belonged to Goldschmidt-Pržibram in Brussels; it was auctioned by Müller in Amsterdam on June 17/19 1924.

78–79. A Court Official of King Henry VIII and his Wife. Double portrait formerly on the lid and on the bottom of a box. Inscribed and dated: ETATIS SVÆ 30 · ANNO 1534 and: ETATIS SVÆ 28 · ANNO 1534. Oil and tempera on limewood. Diam. 4¾ each. *Vienna, Kunsthistorisches Museum.* PLATES 121–122

The man wears the livery of the court with the initials H(enricus) R(ex) sewn on; the woman with white cap and shawl is very similar to the man on the portrait (*Catalogue No.* 80); she is not an Englishwoman but probably Flemish, for which reason it has been suggested that she may be the miniature painter Suzanne, the sister of Lucas Horebout, who married John Parker, the archer and bodyguard of the King. Albrecht Dürer bought one of her miniatures during his journey to the Netherlands in 1521 and judged her age about 18, which, however, was not correct (cf. *Chamberlain, Hans Holbein the Younger, II, p. 70/71*).

In 1806 the two small pictures came to the Imperial Collection in Vienna from Schloss Ambras in the Tyrol.

80. A Court Official of King Henry VIII. About 1534. Oil and tempera on wood. Bottom of a wooden box. 3¾ diam. *Formerly Thonon, Chateau de Ripaille, Coll. Engel-Gros.* PLATE 120

The red beret suggests that the man portrayed was a painter in the service of Henry VIII and, to judge by his appearance, of German or Flemish origin. The idea that he might be the miniature painter Lucas Horebout, who, like his father and sister, worked for the English court, is plausible because, according to tradition, Holbein is supposed to have learnt the art of miniature painting from him. This wooden box, like the contemporary one in Vienna, must have contained a second portrait, that of the artist's wife Marguerite, as pendant.

From a private collection in Paris the picture came into the possession of Mr. F. Engel-Gros at Château de Ripaille near Thonon and in 1891 was exhibited for the first time in Basle (cf. *P. Ganz, KdK.* and *Les portrait miniatures de Hans Holbein le Jeune* in *Revue de l'art ancien e moderne, vol. XXXIX, 1921* and *L'œuvre d'un amateur d'art La Collection de M. F. Engel-Gros, Geneva 1925, p. 124 ff.*) The Fitzwilliam Museum in Cambridge owns a good copy on copper, showing him with a black skull cap and without the royal livery.

81. Thomas Cromwell, Master of the Jewelhous (1490–1540). 1533/34. Half-length figure seated at table, turning three-quarters to the left. Oil and tempera on wood. 29⅞ × 24. *New York, Frick Collection.*

PLATE 125 (126

The sitter, the son of a Putney shoesmith, became Councillor of the King in 1531 and Master of the Jewelhouse in 1532; in 1534 he was secretary to Henry VIII, knighted in 1536, invested with the Order of the Garter in 1537, and made Lord Chancellor and Earl of Essex in 1539. He was executed in 1540 because he was regarded as the chief advocate for the king's marriage to Anne of Cleves and for a protestant policy. The letter on the table is headed: 'To our trusty and right well beloved counsillor Thomas Cromwell, Master of our Jewelhouse.' It follows from this that the portrait must have been painted in the spring of 1534 at latest. The scroll with the inscription praising Cromwell was a later addition and has been removed. The painting was formerly in the collection of the Earl of Arundel and later belonged to the Earl of Caledon at Tyttenhange Park.

A second version of similar size and execution, painted on oak, is in the Chichester-Constable collection in Burton-Constable near Hull; it belonged at one time to Sir Ralph Sadler (1507–1587), who was Cromwell's right-hand man in the dissolution of the monasteries. It remained at his country house at Standon-Lordship Herts., until 1748, when it was inherited by the Aston family, who were ancestors of the present owners.

Neither version now shows the original state; both have been distorted by cleaning and overpainting; certain parts are of excellent quality but it is no longer possible to prove their authenticity even though both can be traced back to two secretaries of Cromwell. It may be that the original has disappeared and that the two portraits given by Cromwell to his companions were executed under Holbein's supervision.

An old copy in the National Portrait Gallery in London shows the original condition without the scroll band at the top. Various copies of the picture are extant (National Portrait Gallery, London; Bell, Oxford), also partial copies as busts (Dr. Hermann, Prague), as a small roundel (Metropolitan Museum, New York) and as a miniature (Sir Walter Blount). Cromwell himself had some of these copies made and distributed amongst his favourites as well as the portrait medal, for which Holbein certainly did the drawing (For possible copyists see *P. Ganz, An English Portrait Painter in Holbein's Atelier* in *Art in America, vol, X, June 1922, p. 153 ff.*).

The portrait painted three or four years later, on which Cromwell is given in half-length only with a roll in his hand and with short whiskers, was also copied several times, sometimes with and sometimes without the Order of the Garter, so that it must be assumed that he had a particular interest in distributing his portrait.

According to *Cust* and *Chamberlain (Burlington Magazine, XX, 1911, pp. 5 and 175)*, a miniature now in the Pierpont Morgan Collection may have been a New Year's present from Holbein to Cromwell in 1538 (cf. *Catalogue No 137*).

82. WOMAN WITH WHITE LINEN COIF. 1533/34. Oil and tempera on oak. $9\frac{1}{8} \times 7\frac{1}{2}$. Detroit, Edsel B. Ford Collection.
PLATE 123

Judging by her un-English appearance and her costly jewelry, the woman seated on an oak bench may have been the wife of the goldsmith Hans of Antwerp, with whom Holbein was in constant contact.

The picture turned up in 1937 in an English private collection and was first published by *Campbell Dodgson (A New Portrait of an English Woman by Holbein* in *Burlington Magazine, September, 1928, p. 105.* cf. also *P. Ganz, A note on a Holbein Portrait* in *Art Quarterly I, No. 2, Spring 1938)*.

83. RICHARD MABON, DEAN OF THE PARISH CHURCH OF ST. HELIER, JERSEY. 1533/34. Oil and tempera on oak. $17 \times 13\frac{3}{8}$. Enschede, Holland, Rijksmuseum Twenthe.
PLATE 124

Mabon was an unusual person, an active administrator and a worker of miracles—so the chronicle reports. He undertook a journey to the Holy Land, to which the cross on his coat is probably an allusion, and carried a seal with the device of the Knights of the Temple. He filled the office of Dean of the parish church four times and built the Jerusalem chapel on the Aoge-Bie (cf. *N. V. L. Rybot, The seals of the Deanery of Jersey* in *St. Helier's Parish Church Magazine, November, 1930)*.

The picture appeared on the Amsterdam market in 1931.

84. UNKNOWN GENTLEMAN WITH MUSIC BOOKS AND A LUTE. 1534/36. Oil and tempera on wood. $17\frac{1}{8} \times 17\frac{1}{8}$. Berlin, Deutsches Museum.
PLATE 127

The picture was described in 1855 as a portrait of the poet and musician Nicolas, Lord Vaux of Harrowden, but a comparison with the two portrait studies at Windsor Castle (*Ganz, C.R. 85* and *C.4; Parker, W. Dr. 24, 30*) shows that this identification is untenable. Nor is the proof convincing that the person represented could be Jean de Dinteville. The portrait drawing discovered by *Miss Mary Hervey* at Chantilly, which she called Jean de Dinteville, shows much similarity to the present portrait but bears little resemblance to the head of Dinteville in the *Ambassadors* or to the drawing at Windsor, which is also supposed to represent him (cf. *Ganz, C.R. 91*) That the sitter is a Frenchman is apparent not only from the elegant attire but also from the face. *H. A. Schmid* dates the painting as early as 1532/35; *Waetzoldt* places it at the very end of Holbein's activity and identifies the man with Jean de Dinteville (cf. *W. Waetzoldt, Hans Holbein d. J., Berlin, 1939, p. 219)*.

The painting is probably identical with the one mentioned in the catalogue of the Arundel Collection, in which it is described as 'Ritratto d'un musico'. It belonged formerly to Sir John Ramsden at Bulstrode Park, who acquired it at an auction in 1860. After 1912 it came into the collection of Henry Goldman, New York, and later by exchange to the Deutsches Museum (cf. *P. Ganz* in *Burlington Magazine, XX, 1911, p. 31)*.

85. CHARLES DE SOLIER, SIRE DE MORETTE (1480/81–1564). 1534/35. Oil and tempera on oak. $36\frac{1}{2} \times 29\frac{5}{8}$. Dresden, Staatliche Gemäldegalerie.
PLATE 129

Charles de Solier came of a Piedmontese family from Asti; as diplomat and soldier he was in the service of four French kings. He was steward and advisor to Francis I, fought at Marignano, and went as ambassador to England in April 1534, where he remained until July 1535. The picture must have been painted during that time at the French embassy at Bridgeville, where Holbein had already painted his two predecessors in 1533. The attitude, the glove on the left hand and the half-covered medallion on the chain recall Titian's 'Homme au Gant' in the Louvre. Morette, as he is named briefly in the documents, wears a cap badge with the picture of John the Baptist and an inscription: DOCE ME FACERE VOLVNTATEM. The gold buttons are adorned with an ornamental motive made of two M's. The preliminary drawing of the head is in the print-room in Dresden (*Ganz, C.R. 38*); an engraving by Wenzel Hollar (*P. 1470, Davidson 596*) seems to have been made from the drawing and gives in addition to the date, 1647, the name 'Mr. Morett, ex collectione Arundeliana.'

The painting came into the possession of Duke Francis I of Modena, after the Earl of Arundel had tried in vain to buy it.

In 1657 the *Microcosmo della Pittura* by Scanelli still mentioned Holbein's picture though the name of the man portrayed was no longer known. Later the name of the artist, too, was forgotten and the painting entered the Dresden gallery of Augustus the Strong as a portrait of Ludovico il Moro, Duke of Milan, by Leonardo da Vinci. Not till the nineteenth century did *Rumohr* recognize it as a work by Holbein and *von Quandt* identified the man as the goldsmith Morett, who had worked at the same time as Holbein at the court of Henry VIII. In 1881, after the Holbein exhibition at Dresden, the Norwegian *M. S. Larpent* published a well documented study, in which he proved that the life-size painting represented the French diplomat. Final proof and the means of dating the portrait were provided by the boxwood model of a medallion by Christopher Weiditz in the British Museum which represents Morette full face, aged about 50 (cf. *P. Ganz, Mitteilungen aus den sächsischen Kunstsammlungen, IV, 1913: Das Bildnis des Sire de Morette in der Gemäldegalerie zu Dresden*).

86. UNKNOWN MAN WITH A RED BEARD, BERET AND GLOVES. Inscribed and dated: ANNO DOMI 1535 ETATIS SVÆ 28. Oil and tempera on oak. 12 diam. *New York, Metropolitan Museum (Bache Collection).*   PLATE 128

The sitter, dressed after the latest French fashion, is a Frenchman, probably a member of the French embassy in London. The preliminary drawing has been preserved at Windsor Castle (*Ganz, C.R. 41; Parker, W. Dr. 33*). It is the same size and is done with coloured chalks and body white on pale pink-tinted paper; the portrait reproduces the drawing stroke for stroke. Only the left hand holding the glove has been added.

The painting belonged formerly to the collection of Alice and Arthur Sachs, New York (cf. *A catalogue of Paintings in the Collection of Jules S. Bache, New York 1929* and *Paul Ganz, Ein unbekanntes Herrenbildnis von Hans Holbein d. J. in Jahrbuch für Kunst und Kunstpflege in der Schweiz, 1921/24, p. 293 ff.*).

87. THE MERCHANT DERICH BERCK OF COLOGNE. Inscribed and dated: AN 1536 ÆTA: 30. Oil and tempera on wood, transferred to canvas, 21 × 16¾. *New York, Metropolitan Museum (Bache Collection).*   PLATE 130

On the letter in his left hand is the sitter's name 'Dem Ersamē u(n)d fromen Derik berk to (?) Luden upt. Stahlhoff' together with his motto 'besad dz end' (Think of the end), and his trademark. On a piece of paper nearby is a second saying: 'Olim meminisse juvabit' (*Aeneid I, 203*).

The painting passed from the collection of the Earl of Egremont into the possession of Lord Leconfield at Petworth where there is a record of it from the beginning of the nineteenth century, and later, through Duveen, to Jules S. Bache, New York (cf. *P. Ganz, Two Unpublished Portraits by Holbein* in *Burlington Magazine, XX, 1911, p. 93*). In 1899 a copy of the painting entered the Alte Pinakothek in Munich from France (*KdK. 219*).

88. SIR RICHARD SOUTHWELL (1504–1563/64). 1536. Dated and inscribed: Xº IVLII · ANNO / H (enrici) VIII · XXVIIIº and ETATIS SVÆ / ANNO XXXIII. Oil and tempera on oak. *Florence, Uffizi.* 18¾ × 15.   PLATE 131

Richard Southwell played a traitor's part in the action against Sir Thomas More and the young Earl of Surrey. Under Cromwell he took part in the dissolution of the monasteries and in the confiscation of Church property in 1535–39. In 1539 he was M.P. for Norfolk and was knighted in 1542. He figured as one of the executors of Henry VIII's will.

The study for the portrait is at Windsor Castle (*Ganz, C.R. 45; Parker, W.Dr. 38*).

The portrait belonged to the Earl of Arundel and was presented by him to the Grand Duke Cosimo II of Tuscany in 1620 (cf. the interesting correspondence in *Rivista d'Arte, VI, 5–6, 1909*).

An excellent replica of the portrait is in the Louvre. Other copies exist, amongst them several without the hands and one with a landscape background in a private collection in Rio de Janeiro.

89. SIR THOMAS STRANGE OR LE STRANGE OF HUNSTANTON (1493–1545). Formerly inscribed and dated: ANNO Dᵉ 1536 AETATIS SUAE 43. Oil and tempera on wood, 15½ × 10½. *Unknown private collection in America (formerly Knoedler and Co. Inc., New York).*   PLATE 132

Le Strange was in the service of King Henry VIII, was knighted in 1520 and became High Sheriff of Norfolk in 1532. He was a cousin of Sir Henry Guildford and married to Anna, sister of Lord Vaux, both of whom were portrayed by Holbein.

The inscription on the blue background was presumably originally on the frame of the portrait and was removed during the recent cleaning.

The preliminary drawing with the eyes looking in a different direction is at Windsor Castle (*Ganz, C.R. 43; Parker, W.Dr. 43*).

The portrait became known through the exhibition of Early English Portraiture in the Burlington Fine Arts Club in 1909 (cf. *Catalogue of the Exhibition. p, 89, pl. XII*). An old copy with a grey-green background still belongs to the family.

90. LADY ELIZABETH VAUX OF HARROWDEN (1505/15–1556). Oil and tempera on wood. 14½ × 11. *Hampton Court, H.M. The King.*   FIGURES 23–24

Lady Elizabeth was a daughter of Sir Thomas Cheyney; her husband Thomas, second Baron Vaux of Harrowden, a cousin of Sir Henry Guildford, also had his portrait painted by Holbein. Until 1536 he was Captain of the Isle of Jersey and died in 1556.

The finished portrait, for which the preliminary drawing is at Windsor Castle (*Ganz, C.R. 86; Parker, W.Dr. 25*), exists in two versions approximately of equal size; one is at Hampton Court Palace, the other in the National Gallery in Prague (Figs. 25–26). X-ray photo-

FIGS. 23-24 (Cat. No. 90). LADY VAUX, Hampton Court, and X-ray photograph
Reproduced by gracious permission of H.M. The King

FIGS. 25-26 (Cat. No. 90). LADY VAUX, Prague Gallery, and X-ray photograph

graphs of both pictures show conclusively that the version at Hampton Court is the overpainted original and that the Prague painting, which was in any case suspect because of the crackle, is a later copy. A miniature painted from the picture is dated 1535.

91. JOHN GODSALVE (about 1510–1555) SITTING ON A WOODEN SEAT. About 1536. Signed on the bottom right: H.H. Oil and tempera on oak. 12⅞ × 9¾. *Philadelphia, Fine Art Museum (John G. Johnson Collection).* PLATE 133

John Godsalve, whom Holbein had already painted with his father in 1528, seems to have renewed contact with the artist after the latter's return to London and to have secured the first commissions for him. He had been in Cromwell's service since 1532 as secretary and clerk of the signet; later, at the accession of Edward VI, he was knighted in 1547. In 1550 he was made Comptroller of the Mint.

The portrait, like the drawing at Windsor Castle, which latter was later coloured with water-colours, gives him in half-length, turned three-quarters to the right (*Ganz, C.R. 62; Parker W.Dr. 22*). It was formerly regarded as an old copy but X-ray photographs have established its authenticity and, revealed the old overpainted signature (cf. *P. Ganz* in *Burlington Magazine, XXVI, 1914, p.47 ff.*).

92. ELIZABETH WIDMERPOLE, WIFE OF JOHN GODSALVE, SITTING ON A WOODEN SEAT. About 1536/38. Inscribed H.H. at the back of the seat on the right. Oil and tempera on oak. 11¾ × 9¾. *Winterthur, Collection Oskar Reinhardt.* PLATE 134

Ludwig Goldscheider suggested to me that the portrait may be the pendant to the portrait of John Godsalve (*Catalogue No. 91*). Picture space and pose correspond as do also the measurements except for a trifling decrease in height. The lady is sitting on the same seat as Godsalve and the same rarely used signature H.H. occurs.

The portrait was described and illustrated for the first time in the catalogue of the exhibition of Early English Portraiture, Burlington Fine Arts Club, 1909 (p. 112, Plate XXIV). Because of the likeness *H. A. Schmid* suggested that the sitter might be a relative or sister of Lady Henegham (cf. his article in *Emanuel Stickelberger, Heisst ein Haus zum Schweizerdegen, vol. II, p. 22 ff.*). He dated it 1537 (*Thieme-Becker*), later 1539.

The picture formerly belonged to the Marquess of Zetland, London.

93. UNKNOWN YOUNG MAN, PROBABLY A HANSEATIC MERCHANT OF THE LONDON STEELYARD. Dated and inscribed: ANNO 1537 ETATIS SV. . . . (cut at the right and redrawn). Oil and tempera on oak. 15⅜ × 12½. Original size about 16½ × 13¼. *Paris, Joseph Schaefer.* FIGURE 27

The features of the man and his dress show a striking likeness to the portrait of an unknown man dated 1541 in the Kunsthistorisches Museum in Vienna (*KdK.115, pl. 145*); it may be the same person a few years younger.

The portrait which belonged formerly to an Austrian

FIG. 27 (Cat. No. 93). UNKNOWN YOUNG MAN

nobleman, appeared on the Berlin market and expert opinions were given by *Bode* and *Friedländer*. The overpainting was removed by Professor Hauser and it was brought into its present state by restoration. It was purchased in 1927 by the present owner.

94–95. DOUBLE PORTRAIT OF KING HENRY VIII AND JANE SEYMOUR. Probably identical with a diptych described as follows in the 1547 inventory of Henry VIII's paintings: 'Item a table like a booke with the picture of kynge Henry theight and Quene Jane' (*Chamberlain, II, p. 109*).

The first mention of Holbein as court painter is in a letter sent from Paris by the French poet Nicholas Bourbon to the king's secretary Thomas Solimar in London in the spring of 1536.

94. KING HENRY VIII. 1536. Oil and tempera on wood in finest miniature painting. 11 × 7½. *Lugano, Baron Thyssen's Family Bequest.* PLATE 135

The painting was done shortly after the king's marriage to Jane Seymour in May 1536 and seems to have been a test in which Holbein revealed the full power of his ability in order to gain the patronage of Henry VIII, from whom he had not yet received any commissions. Success was not slow in coming, for Holbein was appointed to paint the Privy Chamber in Whitehall.

The portrait formerly belonged to Earl Spencer at Althorp; there is a copy in the National Portrait Gallery in London.

95. QUEEN JANE SEYMOUR, THIRD WIFE OF KING HENRY VIII (1509?–1537). 1536. Oil and tempera on wood 10¾ × 7⅜. *The Hague, Mauritshuis.* PLATE 136

Jane Seymour was the eldest daughter of John Seymour of Wolfhall; she came to court in 1530 and was lady-in-waiting both to Catherine of Aragon and to Anne Boleyn. Her marriage was celebrated the day after the execution of her predecessor. She presented the king with an heir to the throne but died at his birth.

Until a few years ago, owing to the heavy overpainting, it was not possible to recognize the picture as an original (*KdK. 195*). In jewelry and dress it is closer to Holbein's preliminary drawing at Windsor Castle (*Ganz, C.R. 44; Parker, W.Dr. 39*) than is the portrait in Vienna and it is probably the identical portrait that Carel van Mander saw at Warmoesstraat in Amsterdam in 1604 and described as an original work. In the *Mauritshuis Catalogue* of 1935 it is assumed that the portrait was brought to Holland from England by William III. Later it belonged to the Prince of Orange-Nassau, whose seal is on the back. It is not, however, included in the list of paintings claimed by Queen Anne. Copies of the picture are at Woburn Abbey, Dalkeith Castle, and in the collection of Lord Sackville at Knole, Kent. A miniature copy with the bust of the queen and the king as pendant in a tortoise-shell box, which was exhibited at the Holbein exhibition of 1871 at Dresden, is inscribed and dated: AÑO · DM̄ · 1536 · AETATIS · SUAE 23.

96. KING HENRY VIII, 1537. Oil and tempera on wood. 39½ × 29½. Contemporary copy. *Windsor Castle, H.M. The King.* PLATE 137

From the many copies of the various portraits of the king it is possible to determine two paintings belonging to this period which show him, not in three-quarters view as the small painting of 1536 and the cartoon for the wall painting (Pl. 214), but facing to the front. In both pictures he wears a red doublet richly embroidered with gold instead of the white one, and a surcoat of red velvet with gold-embroidered borders instead of the gold brocade one; the latter has already been changed in the cartoon for the wall-painting.

The portrait in full-length was used for the Whitehall wall painting; the second, of knee-length only, may have been intended as a pendant to the portrait of Queen Jane Seymour in Vienna. The pose is the same but there are alterations in the dress, in the jewelry and in the weapons. On the wallpainting the king wears a surcoat trimmed with sable and a double row of gold encased rubies as buttons. On the knee-length portrait the surcoat is trimmed with ermine and the doublet has one row of buttons only. The chain hanging over the shoulders appears again on the portrait of 1539/40.

A replica of the portrait presented by the king himself to Sir James Worsley, Governor of the Isle of Wight, belongs to the Earl of Yarborough, Brocklesby Park, Harbrough.

97. QUEEN JANE SEYMOUR, THIRD WIFE OF HENRY VIII (1509?–1537). 1536. Oil and tempera on wood. Formerly strips added to both sides. 25½ × 16. *Vienna, Kunsthistorisches Museum.* PLATE 138

The preliminary drawing at Windsor Castle (*Ganz, C.R. 44; Parker, W.Dr. 39*) gives the bust in the same size but with variations in the jewelry and dress. The wall painting at Whitehall showed the queen in full-length in a state gown richly trimmed with ermine.

The painting was formerly in the Arundel Collection, where it was engraved in the round by Wenzel Hollar (P. 1427, Davidson 570). As early as 1720 it was at the Vienna Hofburg. It was restored in 1937 to its original condition.

98. PRINCESS CHRISTINE OF DENMARK, WIDOWED DUCHESS OF MILAN (1521–1590). 1538. Oil and tempera on wood. 70⅛ × 32. *London, National Gallery.* PLATE 139 (140)

Christine of Denmark was a daughter of King Christian II and Isabella of Spain, sister of Emperor Charles V. The first portrait of the youthful Christine showing her with her brother and sister was painted in 1526 at Malines by Mabuse (now at Hampton Court). When scarcely fifteen years old the princess was married to Duke Francesco Maria Sforza and after his early death she moved to the court of the Austrian Regent Maria of Hungary in Brussels.

Holbein was attached to the mission sent by Henry VIII in March 1538 to discuss the project of a marriage, in order to paint the portrait of the princess, which he is said to have finished in three hours. In spite of Henry's efforts the marriage did not take place and Christine married Duke Francis of Lorraine in 1541.

Obviously the full-length portrait was only executed in London from a study. The preliminary study has not been preserved but a small bust at Windsor Castle, showing slight alterations, may possibly be the original one touched up later, or a copy of it. Both paintings are mentioned in the inventories of Henry VIII in 1542 and 1547.

The full-length portrait was at Lumley Castle in 1597, where it was recorded in the inventory as 'Afterwards Duchess of Lorraine'. The paper with the inscription was only painted in at that time. The picture, acquired by Philip Howard, the father of the Earl of Arundel, remained in the Howard family until 1909, when it was bought by the National Gallery for £60,000.

99. LORD CHANCELLOR THOMAS CROMWELL (1485/90–1540). About 1538. Half-length figure with hands facing three-quarters to the left. Oil and tempera on oak. 20 × 17. *Indianapolis, G. H. A. Clowes Collection.* FIGURE 28

The Lord Chancellor, shown in a similar pose as on his earlier portrait, has a fuller face and thin, greying whiskers. He wears a surcoat with high fur trimming and a black cap with ear flaps. After removal of the heavy overpainting, the picture, cut down on three sides, revealed the original under-drawing, which was done

FIG. 28 (Cat. No. 99). THOMAS CROMWELL

with vigorous pen strokes in Indian ink on a light red-tinted chalk ground.

According to *Chamberlain, II, 58–62*, an expense sheet of Cromwell's includes a payment made to Holbein on 4th January, 1538: 'Hanns the painter 40s' (cf. *Lionel Cust, Burlington Magazine, XX, October 1911, p. 5/6*), which may refer to this portrait.

100. UNKNOWN MAN OF ABOUT 30 YEARS WITH A BLACK BERET. The date 1538 on the frame. Oil and tempera on oak. 19⅝ × 14¼. *Geneva, private collection.*   PLATE 141

The man appears to be one of the protestant courtiers who enjoyed the king's favour and were selected for negotiations with the German princes against Charles V. He holds a dormouse in his hand. Date, age and device are painted on the frame in gold majuscule letters: ANO 1538 (above), ANO ÆTATIS 30 (below), STI (SI) DOMINVS NOBISCVM QVIS CONTRA NOS (St. Paul's Epistle to the Romans 8, 31). Cf. fig. 29.

The painting is from an English collection and came on the art market in 1938 (Illustrated *Kuhn, German Paintings in American Collections, 1936, No. 373, pl. LXXVIII*).

101. A HANSEATIC MERCHANT OF THE STEELYARD IN LONDON. Inscribed and dated: ANNO DOM 1538, AETATIS SVÆ 33. Oil and tempera on oak. 19½ × 15½. *New York, Dr. A. Hamilton Rice.*   PLATE 142

The man wears a signet ring on the first finger of his right hand, which shows a white bar laid diagonally on a black ground and a bird with spread wings standing on the bar as crest.

The portrait was formerly in the collection of Count Kossakowski in Warsaw and came to Paris in 1923. An ancestor of the Count had bought it in 1789 from Gabriel Faszycki, who in his turn had purchased it from the Royal Polish Picture Gallery (cf. *A. L. Mayer in Beiträge zur Geschichte der Deutschen Kunst 1924, I, p. 260/61* and *Valentiner and McCall, Masterpieces of Art, New York World's Fair, 1939, p. 96, No. 199, pl. 44*).

102. CHARLES BRANDON, DUKE OF SUFFOLK (1485–1545). 1540/41. Oil and tempera on oak, 34½ × 29¼. *Present whereabouts unknown (formerly Gallery Norbert Fischman, London).*   PLATE 143

Charles Brandon was educated with Henry VIII and served him successfully as general and statesman until his death. In 1511 he was made Marshal of the King's Household, in 1513 Knight of the Garter, in 1514 Duke of Suffolk. In 1518 he secretly married Mary Tudor, Henry VIII's sister, the dowager queen of France, who bore him two daughters. In 1523 he was Commander-in-Chief of the English army in France and in 1536 he suppressed the 'Pilgrimage of Grace'.

Suffolk commissioned various other works from Holbein for instance the two miniatures of the sons of his fourth wife, now at Windsor Castle, a family group for which the preliminary study still exists (*Ganz, C.R. 100*), and a seal (*Ganz, C.R. 387*).

The painting, several copies of which are extant, formerly belonged to the Marquess of Hastings at Donnington, later to Lady Laudon in Scotland. The old frame bears the inscription: CHAROLVS DVX SVFFVLCIAE SERE' ANGLIAE REGIS R–C ARCHIPREFECTVS CVRIAE (cf. *P. Ganz, A Rediscovered Portrait of Charles Brandon, Duke of Suffolk, by Holbein* in *Burlington Magazine, LVII, August, 1930, p. 59 ff.*).

103. THOMAS HOWARD, DUKE OF NORFOLK (1473–1554). 1539/40. Overpainted inscription on either side of the head: THOMAS DVKE · OFF · NORFOLK · MARSHALL · / AND · TRESURER · OFF · INGLONDE · / THE · LXVI · YERE · OF · HIS · AGE. Oil and tempera on wood. 31¾ × 24. *Windsor Castle, H.M. The King.*   PLATE 144

Thomas Howard, whose wife Anna was a daughter of Edward IV, was uncle by marriage to Henry VIII and to two queens. After Cromwell's fall he became, next to the king, the most influential man in the country but could not prevent the execution in 1547 of his son, the poet Henry Howard. He himself only avoided the same fate thanks to the king's death on the very morning of the day appointed for his execution.

In the portrait he holds in his right hand the Grand Marshall's gold baton and in his left hand the white wand of office as Lord High Treasurer. Round his shoulders is the collar of the Order of the Garter.

The portrait was formerly in the collection of the Earl of Arundel and appears on Fruytier's family portrait, painted from a study by Van Dyck, on the wall of the room (Fig. 31). It was engraved by Vorsterman, noted in the inventory of Arundel's widow in 1655, sold to Holland in 1732 and bought by the Prince of Wales before 1750. A good, old copy is in the possession of the Duke of Norfolk.

104. SIMON GEORGE OF QUOCOTE. About 1540. Oil and tempera on wood. Formerly cut down to form a rectangle but today restored to its original state as a roundel. 12¼ diam. *Frankfurt am Main, Städelsches Kunstinstitut.*

PLATE 145

Through his marriage to Thomasine, daughter of Richard Lanyon, Simon George of Quocote came into contact with the Lanyons of Cornwall.

On the drawing at Windsor Castle (*Ganz, C.R. 61; Parker, W.Dr. 35*), which has been touched up later with pen and Indian ink, the inscription describes him as S. George of Cornwall. The view of the left profile is the same as on the finished portrait but the beard and moustache do not correspond; the features, too, are more pronounced in the drawing.

105. EDWARD, PRINCE OF WALES, LATER KING EDWARD VI (1537–1553). 1539. Oil and tempera on wood. 22⅛ × 17⅞. *Washington, National Gallery (Mellon Collection).*

PLATE 146

The picture is probably the one that Holbein presented to the king on January 1, 1540, and which is listed under the New Year presents as: 'By Hanse Holbeyne a Table of the pictour of the prince (prince's) grace,' for which in return he was presented with a silver gilt drinking glass by the goldsmith Cornelis Hayes.

The preliminary drawing is at Windsor Castle (*Ganz, C.R. 47; Parker, W.Dr. 46*). The distichs in Latin, added later, in which the son is encouraged to surpass his father in virtue and ability and to become the greatest ruler, were composed by the court poet Richard Morysin.

The portrait, which came from a royal Hanoverian collection, was stored for a long time in the Landes-Museum in Hanover and came later into the collection of A. W. Mellon in Pittsburg. Copies of the portrait belong to the Duke of Norfolk, to the Earl of Yarborough, to the National Portrait Gallery and, as a miniature by Peter Olivier, to the collection of the Duke of Devonshire. The Earl of Yarborough's was etched in 1650 in the Arundel Collection by Wenzel Hollar (P. 1395).

106. KING HENRY VIII IN WEDDING DRESS. 1539/40. Inscribed: ANNO · ÆTATIS · SVÆ · XLIX. Oil and tempera on oak. 34¾ × 29½. Replica. *Rome, National Gallery.* PLATE 147

The original, which has disappeared, seems in the first place to have been a pendant to the portrait of Anne of Cleves in the Louvre. The King is wearing the same surcoat of gold brocade with sable as he is on the portrait of 1536 and the same gold-embroidered doublet with jewel trimmings as on the knee-length one at Windsor Castle; the lower part of the dress, however, is embroidered with gold scroll work instead of with the Gothic pattern.

According to a description of the wedding, which took place on 6th January, 1540, at the royal chapel at Greenwich, sent by a foreign ambassador to his government, the king and queen wore for this ceremony the same clothes as on the two portraits.

At one time I regarded the picture as an original; but since I had the opportunity of examining the surface of the painting and noting certain mistakes, such as the way the chain was laid across the shoulders, I have come to the conclusion that it is not a work by Holbein. The picture was formerly in the Galeria Corsini in Rome.

107. QUEEN ANNE OF CLEVES, FOURTH WIFE OF KING HENRY VIII (1515–57). 1539/40. Oil and tempera on parchment, mounted on canvas. Cut down at both sides. 25⅝ × 19. *Paris, Louvre.* PLATE 148

Holbein portrayed the princess in the same position as the dowager Duchess of Milan one year earlier. The portrait is said to have been painted in July 1539 at Schloss Düren, where Holbein had been sent to paint the two daughters of the Duke of Cleves. The unusual material for a picture of this size may have been chosen with a view to its transport and explains the miniature-like execution by means of which, particularly in the rendering of the eyes, Holbein achieved an astonishing vitality.

The marriage with the protestant duchess, made for political reasons, lasted only six months, for the king felt a physical repulsion for the 'Flanders mare' as he called the princess; after the divorce she lived with her own court as Princess Royal at Richmond.

The painting was in the Arundel Collection, where it was etched in 1648 by Wenzel Hollar (P. 1343); after the Earl's death it was put up for sale and passed into the collection of Louis XIV.

108. THOMAS FIENNES LORD DACRE (1517–1541). Inscribed and dated on the frame: 1540 / ÆTATIS 24 · *Ottawa, National Gallery of Canada.* FIGURE 30

Known from a copy reproduced in the portrait of the sitter's wife, Lady Mary Nevill Baroness Dacre, a daughter of George Lord Abergavenny, painted in 1554/55 by Hans Eworth. This shows Holbein's portrait hanging on a tapestry wall of her living room in the original frame of the type used by the artist in his last years (cf. *Lionel Cust, The Painter HE (Hans Eworth), London 1913,* in *Annual of the Walpole Society, II, p. 1–44*).

109. YOUNG MAN WITH REDDISH BEARD AND BLACK BERET. About 1540. Oil and tempera on oak. 16½ × 13⅛. *New York, Aquavella Gallery.* FIGURE 32

In the colour effect of the black-dressed man against an azure blue background the portrait, painted in 1540, shows Holbein's simplified style. Over-cleaning and later restorations, however, have robbed it of its linear precision.

The picture was discovered in England in 1937 and has been sold, via Vienna, to America.

FIG. 29 (Cat. No. 100). UNKNOWN MAN. Cf. Plate 141   FIG. 30 (Cat. No. 108). LORD DACRE

FIG. 31 (Cat. Nos. 103 and 122). FRUYTIERS: GROUP PORTRAIT OF THE ARUNDEL FAMILY, with Holbein's portraits of Henry Howard, Earl of Surrey, and of Thomas Howard, Duke of Norfolk (cf. Plates 144 and 161) on the wall. About 1643

FIG. 32 (Cat. No. 109). YOUNG MAN WITH REDDISH BEARD

110. UNKNOWN LADY OF THE COURT OF HENRY VIII.
1540/43. Inscribed: ANNO ETATIS SVÆ XVII. Oil and tempera on wood. 11¾ × 9¾. *New York, Metropolitan Museum (Bache Collection).*   PLATE 149

The young lady, dressed in the French fashion, wears a locket that may have been designed by Holbein as may also the gold setting for the cameo (cf. *Ganz, C.R. 308/12*).

The painting was formerly in the collection of Count Casimir Lanckoronski in Vienna and came later into the collection of Jules S. Bache, New York (cf. *A Catalogue of the Paintings in the Collection of Jules S. Bache, New York, 1929*).

111. UNKNOWN ENGLISH LADY. 1540/43. Oil and tempera on wood. 7½ × 6. *Vienna, Kunsthistorisches Museum.*
          PLATE 150

The picture is mentioned in the Prague inventory of 1718. The stone window frame, which formerly enclosed the bust, did not belong to the original portrait. In a recent restoration 'these additional pieces stuck on in the eighteenth century, which formed a frame round the lady portrayed' were removed; this reduced height and width by 3 cms. each.

A copy in an English private collection, also showing the stone frame, is inscribed on the back with the name: Anne Chambre wiffe of John Chambre M.D.

112. MARGARET WYATT, LADY LEE. Inscribed: ETATIS SVÆ · 34. About 1540. Oil and tempera on wood. 16¾ × 12⅞. *New York, Metropolitan Museum.*   PLATE 151

Margaret Wyatt, according to a suggestion of *Cust*, was a daughter of Sir Henry Wyatt and the sister of the poet Sir Thomas Wyatt, both of whom were portrayed by Holbein. She was married to Sir Anthony Lee. The name appeared on an old copy belonging to Viscount Dillon of Ditchley, Oxon. The picture belonged to the Palmer family from about 1640 and was published for the first time in *Burlington Magazine, XV, May, 1909*, and in the *Illustrated Catalogue of Early English Portraiture, pl. XXII.* It passed to the Metropolitan Museum with the Benjamin Altman Collection.

113. UNKNOWN GENTLEMAN WITH LETTER AND GLOVES. About 1540. Oil and tempera on wood. 12⅝ × 10. *Basle, Öffentliche Kunstsammlung.*   PLATE 152

The two-line inscription on the letter is no longer legible. *Davies* thought the man represented a London merchant. The picture was purchased in 1862 from a Basle art dealer.

114. MR. DE VOS VAN STEENWIJK FROM HOLLAND. Dated and inscribed: ANNO · 1541 / ETATIS · SVÆ · 37. Oil and tempera on wood. 18½ × 14¼. *Berlin, Deutsches Museum.*
          PLATE 153

Miss Clare Stuart Wortley succeeded in identifying the sitter with the help of the arms on the signet ring. The picture was formerly in the Suermondt collection at Aachen.

115. UNKNOWN YOUNG MAN AT HIS OFFICE DESK. Inscribed and dated: ANNO · DNI · 1541 · ETATIS · SVÆ · 28. Oil and tempera on wood. 18½ × 13¾. *Vienna, Kunsthistorisches Museum.*   PLATE 154

To all appearances the man is a German and may have belonged to the Merchants of the Steelyard.

The picture was formerly owned by the Archduke Leopold Wilhelm. An old copy is in the Palermo gallery.

116. UNKNOWN YOUNG WOMAN WITH A WHITE COIF. Inscribed and dated: ANNO · 1541 ETATIS SVÆ · 19. Oil and tempera on oak. 4⅜ diam. *Los Angeles, County Museum.*   PLATE 155

From an English private owner the portrait came into the collection of Oscar Huldschinsky, Berlin. It is illustrated in the sale catalogue of 1928 as No. 47; later it became the property of Mr. Allen C. Balsh, Los Angeles, and at his death passed to the County Museum (cf. *Los Angeles County Museum Quarterly Magazine, April-September 1943* and *American Art News, December 15, 1944*).

117. LADY ELIZABETH RICH (died 1558). 1541/43. Oil and tempera on oak. 17½ × 13¾. *Basle, Galerie Katz.*

                         PLATE 156

Elizabeth Rich was the daughter of a wealthy London spice merchant; in 1535 she married Sir Richard Rich, Cromwell's procurator-general, who was knighted in 1547/48 and became Lord Chancellor of England. Four sons and ten daughters were the fruits of their union.

Holbein seems to have painted them both at the same time as pendants, for the two preliminary drawings at Windsor Castle are pendants of the same size (*Ganz, C.R. 76; Parker, W.Dr. 55 and 80*). The portrait of the husband has disappeared but that of the wife is preserved in two versions of the same size, both of them over-painted. An X-ray photograph showed that one was the original. It contains a beautifully executed piece of jewelry with a group of men in front of a woman lying dead on the ground, which was certainly designed by Holbein. The right hand is missing in the study.

In the seventeenth century both versions were the property of the Crofts of Croft Castle, and both were inherited by the Moseley family at Buildwas Park, Shropshire, whence 100 years later they came on to the English art market. The second version was aquired by Mr. Altman of New York, with whose collection it passed to the Metropolitan Museum (cf. *Chamberlain, II, p. 212*).

118. QUEEN CATHERINE HOWARD, FIFTH WIFE OF KING HENRY VIII (1520/21–1542). 1540/41. Oil and tempera on oak. 29⅛ × 20⅛. Inscribed: ETATIS SVÆ · 21. *Toledo, U.S.A., Museum of Art.*   PLATE 157

Catherine Howard, a niece of the Duke of Norfolk, came to court at an early age. She was one of the ladies-in-waiting destined for the service of Queen Anne of Cleves. When the marriage, which had been arranged by Cromwell, broke up and the Lord Chancellor was condemned to death, his political rival, the Duke of Norfolk, succeeded in arranging a marriage between his own niece and the king. The tragic end of her cousin Anne Boleyn did not deter her and, as reported by the French ambassador Marillac, during the first part of their marriage Henry was so much in love with her that he could not treat the new queen well enough and caressed her more than any of the others. Happiness did not last long, however, for Catherine was beheaded in the Tower on February 13, 1542, accused of adultery.

The study at Windsor Castle, which until recently had been regarded as the preliminary sketch for a similar portrait, does not, according to *Parker (W.Dr. 62)* represent Catherine Howard. On the other hand, the preliminary drawing for the locket with the representation of Lot's wife turning into a pillar of salt, designed by Holbein, has been preserved in the British Museum (*Ganz, C.R. 290*).

The portrait passed from the collection of Cromwell Bush, London, to that of James Dunn in Canada and finally to Edward Drummond-Libbey (cf. *Toledo Museum of Art Catalogue of the European Paintings 1939*). In

a copy in the National Portrait Gallery in London the embroidery on the pocket, which is less clear in the original, represents God the Father enthroned.

119. KING HENRY VIII IN A WIDE VELVET SURCOAT AND A STICK IN HIS LEFT HAND. Signed and dated on the handle of the stick: H (H) (15) 42. Oil and tempera on oak. 36½ × 26¼. *Castle Howard, York, George Howard, Esq.*

                PLATE 158 (159–160)

The portrait discovered at Castle Howard in 1933 is the prototype for the last group of portraits of the king, in which Henry VIII is already shown in an advanced state of obesity. He is wearing a bell-shaped surcoat of red Venetian velvet, which covers his whole body and hides the disfiguring corpulence, but the puffy features and the thickened fingers betray the symptoms that Mr Joe Geilkie Cobb declared in a letter to *The Times* (October 16, 1933) to be 'signs of thyroid deficiency'.

In spite of three overpaintings of the whole picture, which had to be removed, the original condition has been preserved in all details. The coat alone has lost something of its plastic effect owing to the disappearance of the large folds at the side, which are still visible on the copy at Bethlehem Royal Hospital, Beckenham (Fig. 33). Further copies are at Warwick Castle, the National Portrait Gallery, in the collection of the Marquess of Bute (cf. *P. Ganz in Burlington Magazine, LXIII, 1933, p. 80 ff. and p. 182 ff.*).

FIG. 33 (Cat. No. 119). KING HENRY VIII. Copy showing the original condition. Beckenham, Bethlehem Royal Hospital

As early as 1616 a portrait of the king belonged to the Howards (Carel van Mander) and the portrait can be identified since 1720.

120. Sir George Carew (1514?–1545). 1542/3. Traces of an original inscription (A of ANNO) above the later four-lined one. Oil and Tempera on oak. 13¼ diam. *Weston Park, Shifnal, Earl of Bradford.*   PLATE 163

The man portrayed, a soldier, wears as ornament and cap badge a medal with St. George the dragon killer. In 1540 he was commander of the fortress of Ruysbank near Calais, 1543/44 Lieutenant-General of the Cavalry and in 1545 Commander of H.M.S. *Maryrose*, which sank with all hands aboard when leaving Portsmouth Harbour.

The preliminary drawing is at Windsor Castle (*Parker, W.Dr. 76*); it has been so badly rubbed and touched up that I listed it with the copies in my catalogue of Holbein's drawings (*Ganz, C.R. C.2*).

The present inscription was painted on the blue background after the death of Carew and reads: SIR GEORGE CAREW / KNIGHT FIRST · SOHN TO SIR / WILLM · CAREW DROWNED · AT / PORTSMOUTH IN THE MARYROS /.

121. Unknown Nobleman with a Hawk. Dated and inscribed 1542 · ANNO · ETATIS · SVÆ XXVIII. Oil and tempera on wood. 9⅞ × 7½. *The Hague, Mauritshuis.*
                                                    PLATE 162

The painting went to Holland with the collection of William of Orange and its return was requested in vain by Queen Anne.

122. The Poet Henry Howard, Earl of Surrey (1516/18–1546). 1541/43. Inscribed: HENRY HOWARD ERLE OF SURRY ANNO AETATIS SVÆ 25. Oil and tempera on oak. 21⅞ × 17¾. *New York, Wildenstein & Co.*
                                                    PLATE 161

Henry Howard, called the Earl Poet, was the eldest son of the eighth Duke of Norfolk, a cousin of Henry VIII, Queen Anne Boleyn and Catherine Howard. In 1545/46 he was Commander of Boulogne but was dismissed after a defeat at St. Etienne and in 1547 executed in the Tower for high treason because he quartered his arms with those of the king, a privilege that was his by right.

On the wall of the room represented in the portrait group of the Earl of Arundel and his family, painted on parchment by Fruytiers about 1643 after a sketch by Van Dyck, Henry's picture hangs next to that of his father (cf. Fig. 31); it was also engraved at that time by Wenzel Hollar (P. 1509).

Holbein had already painted the portrait of Henry Howard with his wife Frances, daughter of the Earl of Oxford, in 1533; the two preliminary drawings are at Windsor Castle (*Parker, W.Dr. 17, 18*); a study published by *Parker* as an original in which Howard is given turning three-quarters to the left, provided it is by Holbein or copied from one of his works, must have been done between 1535 and 1542, for the man portrayed is

older than on the full-face study and younger than on the portrait. As I do not know a miniature in the Hawkins Collection, in which Frances is about 23 years old, I can only state that the date of origin could tally with the date of the second study of 1539/40.

123. Sir William Butts the Younger (1513–1570/80). 1543. Dated and inscribed: ANNO · DNI · 1543 · ÆTATIS SVÆ XXX. Oil and tempera on oak. 29⅛ × 23¼. *Boston, Fine Arts Museum.*   PLATE 164

Sir William Butts, a son of Henry VIII's physician, was High Sheriff of Norfolk and Suffolk under Queen Elizabeth. The portrait was probably painted at the same time as the two pendants of his parents (Gardner Museum, Boston). In expectation of a visit from the queen, Butts had his portrait overpainted by a local painter to bring it up to date. The coloured dress, customary under Henry VIII, was replaced by the black court dress worn in Queen Elizabeth's day; at the same time the reddish full beard was altered to a greyish pointed one and the gold chain, which he had received as a favour at the hands of Queen Elizabeth, was added.

In spite of this thorough overpainting, the portrait, an heirloom in the Butts family, was regarded by them as a work by Holbein. It was not, however, generally recognized as such until in 1929, when the property had to be divided up, an X-ray photograph revealed the original condition and thus confirmed the family tradition. From Mrs. Colville-Hyde, the last heir, the picture passed to Boston (cf. *P. Ganz* in *Burlington Magazine, LVI, March, 1930, p. 118 ff.*).

124–125. Double Portrait of the King's Physician, Sir William Butts, and his Wife, Lady Margaret Butts. 1543. Oil and tempera on oak. 18½ × 14½. *Boston, Isabella Stewart Gardner Museum.*   PLATES 165–166

124. Sir William Butts (1484/85–1545). Inscribed: ANNO · ÆTAT[I]S · SVE LIX.

Sir William Butts, the physician of Henry VIII, is described by Shakespeare in *Henry VIII* as the king's confidant (Act V, Scene II). Holbein painted him a second time on the picture in the Barbers' Hall (*Cat. No. 181; Fig. 34*), which was begun in the same year; he appears there in a similar side view, as the second person behind Chambers, kneeling on the right of the throne. A copy is in the National Portrait Gallery in London.

125. Lady Margaret Butts (1486–1545). Inscribed: ANNO · ÆTATIS SVE · LVII.

Lady Margaret Butts was the daughter of John Bacon of Cambridgeshire and met her future husband, Princess Mary's physician, whilst serving the princess as lady-in-waiting. The study at Windsor Castle (*Ganz, C.R. 50; Parker, W.Dr. 67*) is the preliminary drawing for the painting in Boston.

FIG. 34 (Cat. Nos. 124 and 181). SIR WILLIAM BUTTS. Detail from the painting in the Barbers' Hall, London (Plate 218)

The portrait was in the Arundel Collection, where it was etched by Wenzel Hollar (P. 1553).
Both pictures at one time belonged to W. H. Pole Carew.

126. DR. JOHN CHAMBERS. 1543. Inscribed: ÆTATIS SVE. 88. Dated through the guild painting in Barbers' Hall (*Cat. No. 181*). Oil and tempera on oak. 20⅛ × 16⅛. *Vienna, Kunsthistorisches Museum.*   PLATE 167
Chambers was Henry VIII's physician and president of the Barber-Surgeons' Guild; on the painting in Barbers' Hall (*Catalogue No. 181*) he is kneeling on the right of the throne with cap, fur coat and gloves in the same position as on the portrait (Fig. 34). False additions were removed in 1918, thereby reducing the depth by 5½ in. and the width by 2¾ in.
The portrait at one time belonged to the Arundel Collection and was etched by Wenzel Hollar with the inscription: D · CHAMBERS · Holbein pinxit / ANNO AETATIS · SUE 88 (P. 1372). Later it came into the possession of the Archduke Leopold Wilhelm and passed with his collection to the Kunsthistorisches Museum in Vienna.

127. DUKE ANTON THE GOOD OF LORRAINE (1490–1544). Inscribed: ÆTATIS · SVÆ 54; 1543, dated through the indication of the age. Oil and tempera on oak. 20⅛ × 14½. *Berlin, Deutsches Museum.*   PLATE 168
Duke Anton, a soldier of distinction in his youth, was

an invalid in his old age. He was the father of Duke Francis, the second husband of Christine of Denmark.
Oskar Fischel succeeded in establishing the identity of the sitter (cf. *Jahrbuch der preussischen Kunstsammlungen 1926, p. 187*). Although the indication of the age and the artistic perfection suggest the last years of Holbein's life, it is not impossible that he made studies for the portrait as early as 1538, when he had been ordered by Henry VIII to make a portrait of the Duke's daughter Anna at Nancy.
On the back is an old English collector's mark: W.E.P.L.C. (sixteenth century?), which recurs on the back of the Cheseman portrait in The Hague (*Cat. No. 72*). The picture first became known at the Dresden Holbein exhibition in 1871. In 1897 it was purchased for the Berlin collections from the painter Sir John Everett Millais, who had bought it on the London art market.

128. EDWARD PRINCE OF WALES AT THE AGE OF SIX YEARS. 1543. Inscribed: ÆTATIS · SVÆ · VI. Oil and tempera on oak. 12¾ diam. *New York, Metropolitan Museum (Bache Collection).*   PLATE 169
The portrait, discovered by Lord Lee of Fareham in 1922 in a completely overpainted condition, is one of Holbein's last works, for it must certainly have been finished for the prince's birthday October 12, 1543. Although it has suffered some damage it is one of the artist's finest achievements.

Holbein had twice before painted the prince *en face*. In the study with the monkey at Basle (*Ganz, C.R. 48*) he is more of a child than in the other one at Windsor Castle (*Ganz, C.R. 49; Parker, W.Dr. 71*). Both paintings have disappeared but the drawing at Windsor corresponds to two copies (Christ's Hospital, London, and private collection in Scotland), on which the prince is represented half-length facing to the front holding a dagger and his belt with his hands. The same half-length figure in a different dress and with a rose in the right hand can be seen in a copy in the National Portrait Gallery in London. The same motive recurs in a second portrait, of which two versions also exist, a half-length figure in profile (Lord Lytton and National Portrait Gallery). A second drawing at Windsor Castle is connected with this latter portrait (*Parker, W.Dr. 85*). Like the portrait mentioned, it is not by Holbein and the prince is more than six years old (cf. *P. Ganz, The Last Work of Hans Holbein the Younger* in *Apollo, II, No. 12, December 1925; Tancred Borenius, Catalogue of Pictures, Lee Collection, 1923, p. 44 ff.; A Catalogue of Paintings in the Collection of Jules S. Bache, New York, 1929*).

129. PRINCESS MARY, DAUGHTER OF KING HENRY VIII (1516–1558). 1543. Oil and tempera on oak. 14½ diam. *London, Private Collection.* PLATE 170

Mary, the daughter of Henry VIII and his first wife Catherine of Aragon, spent most of her life away from the court. Not till the spring of 1543, thanks to the efforts of Catherine Parr, the sixth Queen, was she acknowledged by her father after a reconciliation and declared to be in the line of succession to the throne. She succeeded Edward VI on his death in 1553 and married Philip II of Spain in 1556.

Like the roundel of Prince Edward, the portrait comes from an unknown collection; it was discovered in 1937 completely overpainted and was restored at the same time, whereby the damage to the collar was revealed and repaired. The identification of the sitter with Princess Mary is based not only on the striking similarity between her profile and that of her brother Edward but also on a comparison with various other portraits. An early one in three-quarters view must have been painted by Holbein during a former, temporary reconciliation in 1536. It is now lost and known only from an etching by Wenzel Hollar with the inscription: Princeps Maria Henrici VIII Regis Angliae filia. H. Holbein pinxit, W. Hollar fecit. ex Collectione Arundeliana 1647 (*Parthey 1465, KdK. 199*). A badly damaged portrait study at Windsor Castle with the inscription 'Lady Mary after Queen' which, owing to its present condition, I did not regard as an original appears to have been the preliminary drawing for Hollar's engraved portrait with the sides reversed.

Recently it has been acknowledged as authentic by *Parker (W.Dr. 41*) and by *H. A. Schmid (Hans Holbein d. J. 113*).

Two other portraits, painted after Holbein's death, are in the National Portrait Gallery, London, and in the Ashmolean Museum, Oxford. The former, dated 1544, gives the princess in front view and shows the same structure of the head and the features, the same slightly hooked nose and the peculiar glance of the eyes as seen on our portrait (Illustrated by *Fletcher and Walker, Historical Portraits 1400–1600, London 1909*). The portrait in the Ashmolean Museum, only a few years later, is very similar (*Catalogue of Early English Portraiture, 1909 No. 36, pl. IX*).

130. SELF-PORTRAIT. Inscribed and dated: H.H. / AN 1542 ÆTA · 45. Oil and tempera on oak. 4⅛ diam. *Indianapolis, U.S.A., Dr. G. H. A. Clowes.* PLATE 171

The roundel, about the size of Holbein's box portraits, is a self-portrait, for which the preliminary drawing was in all probability the one in the collection of artists' portraits in the Uffizi at Florence, now very much altered by later overpainting (*Ganz, C.R. 51*). It is dated a year earlier than the miniatures made from it, which give the same age and the year of Holbein's death, 1543; they were probably not done till after his death.

The artist painted himself in front of an easel with a paint brush in his right hand and a box of colours in his left.

The portrait could be one of the two self-portraits that Carel van Mander saw in Amsterdam (cf. *Catalogue No. 64*), for it was etched as early as 1616 by Vorsterman with the sides reversed. Later it belonged to the von Stackelberg family at Faehna in Estland and finally to the Paravicini-Engel Collection in Basle (cf. *P. Ganz, Das Bildnis Hans Holbeins d. J. in Jahrbuch für Kunst und Kunstpflege in der Schweiz, V, 1928/29, p. 273 ff. and Chamberlain, I, p. 27*).

131. SELF-PORTRAIT. 1542/3. Inscribed: IOANNES HOLPENIVS BA / SILEENSIS / SVI IPSIVS EFFIGIATOR · Æ · XLV. Black and coloured chalk on pink-tinted paper. Measurements without the later additions: 9 × 7⅛. *Florence, Uffizi.* ILL. PAGE 14

The drawing must be regarded as a study for a self-portrait; it shows the same technique as the late drawings at Windsor. After it had been acquired in 1714 by Cardinal Leopold Medici for his collection of artists' portraits it was enlarged on all four sides and almost entirely painted over with water-colour and gold in accordance with the taste of the period. The present inscription conforms to an older one in cursive lettering, a few words of which have been preserved.

III. MINIATURES

The miniature portraits attributed to Holbein are all made from paintings by the artist. The technique is the same throughout: watercolour on paper, cardboard or vellum, blue background and gold inscriptions. Accuracy and precision of the draughtsmanship are the sole factors in determining their authenticity.

According to Carel van Mander, Holbein is supposed to have learnt the art of miniature painting from Lucas Horebout, the son of the miniature painter Gerald Horebout or Horenbolt of Ghent, who in 1537, as court painter, received a salary from Henry VIII. The miniatures known today all belong to the period after 1534 when Holbein was already working for the court.

Heads or half-length figures only are represented, with and without hands, about the size of a portrait medal; the miniatures were generally set as lockets, more rarely preserved in wooden or ivory boxes with screw-down lids.

Cf. also *Carl Winter, Holbein's Miniatures, Burlington Magazine, Nov. 1943, pp. 266 ff.*

---

132. BEARDED YOUNG MAN WITH RED BERET. About 1534/35. Watercolour on a playing card. $1\frac{3}{16}$ diam. *Paris, Collection L. Michelson.*　　　　PLATE 172

Red berets were generally worn by artists.

133. GEORGE NEVILL, LORD ABERGAVENNY. After 1534. Inscribed on the left in cursive lettering: G. Abergaueny. Watercolour on a playing card. $2\frac{1}{8}$ diam. *Drumlanrig Castle, Thornhill, Duke of Buccleuch.*　　PLATE 189

The miniature is made from the portrait (*Cat. No. 75*) the preliminary drawing for which belongs to the Earl of Pembroke (*Ganz, C.R. 37*) and the painting itself to the Erickson collection in New York. The version illustrated here is not by Holbein (cf. *Connoisseur, 1907, XVIII, p. 143* and *Catalogue of Early English Portraiture, 1909. Plate XXXIII, No. 22*).

134–135. WILLIAM ROPER OF WELLHALL AND HIS WIFE MARGARET ROPER. 1536. Inscribed: ANᵒ ÆTATIS SVÆ XLII and: Aᵒ ÆTATIS XXX. Watercolour on cardboard. $1\frac{3}{4}$ diam. *New York, Mrs. Henry Goldman.*　PLATES 175–176

The two pendants represent husband and wife in half-length with hands. They are of exquisite workmanship. Margaret More, Sir Thomas' eldest daughter, is shown in the same pose as on the family portrait but wearing a different dress and holding the closed book in her left hand. Her features are older and more careworn than in the group portrait of 1527/28 and in the copy belonging to Lord Sackville (*KdK. 194*). Formerly Collection of Lord Rothschild, London, later Lord Carnarvon.

136. QUEEN JANE SEYMOUR (1509?–1537). 1536. $1\frac{1}{2}$ diam. Inscribed: ANᵒ XXV. Watercolour on paper. *Charlbury, Cornbury Park, Oxon., Mr. Vernon Watney.*

The miniature was originally the property of the Seymour family. Charles, Duke of Somerset, gave it to his granddaughter Elisabeth Wyndham, wife of the Right Hon. George Granville. Later it passed into the collections of the Duke of Buckingham, of Mr. Sackville Bale and of Dr. Lumsden Propert (Illustrated *KdK. 148* and *Catalogue of Early English Portraiture, Burlington Fine Arts Club, 1908, pl. XXXII, 2*).

Of the four versions known today two belonged to Horace Walpole at Strawberry Hill. On the one (Collection of the Duke of Buccleuch), she is wearing the same jewelry as on the above example, a medallion with the Holy Trinity; on the others a Cross of St. Anthony made of sapphires and a brooch with rubies. The identification seems assured from two miniatures fitted in a box which were exhibited in the Holbein exhibition at Dresden in 1871 and represent Henry VIII and Jane Seymour; the latter is inscribed in gold lettering: A̅N̅O̅ D̅M̅ 1536 AETATIS SVE 23 (*W. II, p. 140, No. 212*). The box came into the collection of Hjalmar Wicander in Stockholm (coloured illustration in *Karl Asplund's catalogue, vol. II, pl. 80*).

137. LORD CHANCELLOR THOMAS CROMWELL, EARL OF ESSEX (1490–1540). After August 1537. Two miniatures in watercolour on cardboard, both in the same gold locket with a richly decorated top. $1\frac{3}{4}$ diam. *London, Art Market.*　　　　PLATES 190–191

The miniatures, head and shoulders turned three-quarters to the left, are derived from two portraits painted by Holbein in 1537/38 after the Earl's investiture with the insignia of the Garter. This rare jewel was auctioned at Christie's in 1932.

A further miniature, in ivory and gold filigree frame set with pearls, also showing the sitter wearing chain and George of the Garter on blue background, belonged at one time to the Pierpont Morgan Collection and was sold with that collection at Christie's in 1932 (sale catalogue No. 137) as a schoolwork of Hans Holbein. Although *Lionel Cust (A newly-discovered miniature of Thomas Cromwell, Burlington Magazine XX, Oct. 1911, p. 526)* regarded it as an original, its authenticity is just as doubtful as that of the first-mentioned pair.

138. THOMAS WRIOTHESLEY, EARL OF SOUTHAMPTON (1494?-1550). 1538? Watercolour on cardboard; high oval. $1\frac{3}{16} \times 1\frac{15}{16}$. *New York, Metropolitan Museum.* PLATE 177

The miniature is copied from a larger portrait for which the preliminary drawing in chalk on pink-tinted paper was acquired from the Fleming Collection for the Louvre in 1919. The original painting is lost.

Thomas Wriothesley took part in the mission sent by Henry VIII in 1538/39 to the Rhine and to Flanders in search of a wife, to which Holbein was attached as portraitist. Later he filled the high office of Lord Chancellor of England and was named by the king as an executor of his will.

139. QUEEN ANNE OF CLEVES (1515-1557). 1539/40. Watercolour on vellum in an ivory box. $1\frac{3}{4}$ diam. *London, Victoria and Albert Museum (Salting Bequest).*

PLATE 178

Bust after the portrait in three-quarters length in the Louvre. In the museum catalogue of 1930 the miniature is listed as an original work by Holbein; it has, however, recently been maintained that it is a copy by a contemporary artist after a painting by Holbein.

For a long time the miniature belonged to the Barrett family at Lee Priory, Kent; in 1757-8 it was auctioned in London and later came into the Collection of George Salting, who bequeathed it to the museum.

140. MRS. PEMBERTON. About 1540. Watercolour on a playing card. Inscribed: ANNO ETATIS SVÆ 23. $2\frac{1}{8}$ diam. Set as a locket in a black and white enamelled gold frame and adorned with three pearls. *London, Victoria and Albert Museum.* PLATE 174

Half-length figure with hands three-quarters to the right. The woman is probably Margaret Pemberton (died 1576), daughter of Richard Throgmorton and wife of Robert Pemberton, whose grandmother on his father's side was the last heir of the Sago di Lago family. Their family arms on the back are quartered with those of Pemberton. According to the date, however, the alliance arms were not added until 1566.

The miniature was formerly in the collections of C. Heywood-Hawkins, C. H. T. Hawkins, and Pierpont Morgan.

141-142. QUEEN CATHERINE HOWARD (1520/21-1542). 1540/42. Watercolour on paper. $2\frac{1}{4}$ diam. *Windsor Castle, H.M. The King.* PLATE 179-180

Pose and attitude, half-length figure with folded hands, correspond to the portrait now in the Toledo Museum of Art (cf. *Cat. No. 118*) but the clothes and jewelry differ. A second version, in which the hands are no longer fully visible, has been cut down all round to 2 diam. (*Thornhill, Scotland, Duke of Buccleuch*). It was engraved by Wenzel Hollar in the collection of the Earl of Arundel, later it belonged to the painter Jonathan Richardson the Younger and to Horace Walpole at Strawberry Hill.

H

143. LADY ELIZABETH AUDLEY. After 1540. Watercolour. $2\frac{3}{16}$ diam. *Windsor Castle, H.M. The King.* PLATE 181

In pose and dress the miniature corresponds to a preliminary drawing for a portrait. It received the title 'The Lady Audley' about 1550 (*Ganz, C.R. 52; Parker, W.Dr. 58*). No painted portrait is known.

It is not possible to identify the lady with certainty because the Christian name is missing on the inscription, which is of a later date. She is probably Elizabeth (Isabell) the first wife of the ninth Lord Audley, George Tuchet, and daughter of Sir Brian Tuke. The lady, however, died as early as 1554 whereas her husband did not inherit the title until 1557.

144. THE PAINTER HARRY MAYNERT. After 1540. Inscribed: H.M. ETATIS SVÆ 27. Watercolour on paper. 2 diam. *Munich, Bavarian National Museum.* PLATE 182

The sitter, at one time identified with the Munich painter Hans Mühlich, is more probably the painter Harry Maynert, who was present on 8 October 1543 as one of the four witnesses to Holbein's will.

The miniature was recognized and published in 1911 by Dr. Buchheit as a work by Hans Holbein (cf. *Ausgewählte Kunstwerke aus dem Bayrischen Nationalmuseum in München 1922, Amt. Ausgabe, Fig. 53*).

145. HENRY BRANDON, SON OF THE DUKE OF SUFFOLK (1535-1551). After 6th September 1540. Inscription on the table: ETATIS SVÆ · 5 · 6 . SEPDEM / ANNO 1535. $1\frac{7}{8}$ diam. *Windsor Castle, H.M. The King.* PLATE 183

The boy was the first son of Duke Charles Brandon by his fourth wife, Catherine Willoughby de Eresby, whom he had married in 1534; the date can only refer to the birthday of the boy which is not otherwise known. Like his brother, the boy fell ill and died very young.

The unusual attitude of the boy, who has his left arm on a table, goes back to a drawing by Holbein (*Ganz, C.R. 100*), in which he is sitting next to his mother or stepsister with his arm resting on a wooden seat. In the drawing he is more vivid and not sentimentally conceived as he is in the miniature, the authenticity of which has rightly been questioned.

This miniature and the following one came into the Collection of King Charles I as a present from one of the dukes of Suffolk.

146. CHARLES BRANDON, SON OF THE DUKE OF SUFFOLK (1538-1551). Inscribed: ANN / 1541 ETATIS SVÆ 3/10 MARCI. $1\frac{7}{8}$ diam. *Windsor Castle, H.M. The King.*

PLATE 184

The miniature, like the pendant, seems to be inscribed with the boy's birthday, 10th March. Charles, the younger son of Brandon's fourth marriage, can be seen on Holbein's portrait group drawing standing at the opposite end of the seat on which his brother is sitting. He is very similar to the miniature, which shows all the characteristics of Holbein's art in its execution.

147. Unknown Youth with short Hair. About 1540. Watercolour on paper. 1⅜ diam. *The Hague, Royal House Archives.*   PLATE 173

The miniature, discovered and attributed to Holbein by *Sir Richard Holmes,* is one of the most perfect works of the master. It portrays, according to *Holmes,* a young Hanseatic merchant of the London Steelyard; *Davies* takes him for a young Englishman (cf. *R. R. Holmes, An unpublished Miniature by Holbein in the Possession of the Queen of Holland, Burlington Magazine, April 1903*).

148. The Hanseatic Merchant Heinrich von Schwarzwald from Danzig. Inscribed and dated: · ANNO · ETATIS · SVÆ 24 · 1 · 5 · 4 · 3. Watercolour on cardboard. 2¼ diam. *Danzig, Stadtmuseum.*   PLATE 185

The man portrayed has the trademark of the Reesen family on his signet ring. He is probably a member of the Danzig patrician family von Schwarzwald, Henry, son of Hans and Grete von Reesen, who occupied the post of juror in Danzig (1517–1561) (cf. *Georg Habich, Ein Miniaturbildnis von Hans Holbein in Danzig,* in *Zeitschrift für bildende Kunst, XXIV, 1913, p. 194ff.*).

The miniature came to the reformed church of St. Peter in 1708 from the Schwarzwald family.

149–151. Self-Portraits in front of his Easel. Inscribed and dated: H / H / A . N 1543 / ETATIS SVE · 4 · 5. Watercolour on playing card or vellum (151). 1 7⁄16 diam. *London, Wallace Collection; Drumlanrig Castle, Thornhill, Duke of Buccleuch; and Antwerp, Museum Mayer van den Bergh.*   PLATE 186–188

The back of the wooden box in which the first miniature is preserved is inscribed 'Hans Holbein given to Me by Lord Bolingbroke 1757'.

The second version was once in the collection of Horace Walpole at Strawberry Hill and was published in *Catalogue of Early English Portraiture, 1909, pl. XXXIII, No. 23.*

The third version is illustrated in the *Catalogue des Tableaux de la collection du chevalier Mayer van den Bergh, No. 185.*

All three miniatures have the same inscription as the hand-sized picture in the Clowes collection, Indianopolis (*Catalogue No. 130*), but the date 1543 is that of the artist's death (cf. *Chamberlain, I, 27–8 and II, 230–1*).

IV. MONUMENTAL AND DECORATIVE WORKS

152. Painted Table for the Standard Bearer Hans Baer of Basle. Inscribed on the seal of the letter: HANS HOLBEIN and dated: 1515. Oil and tempera on pinewood. 3 ft. 4 in. × 4 ft. 5½ in. *Zürich, Schweizerisches Landes-museum.*   PLATE 193 (192, 194–195)

The composition, adapted to the Gothic table top, is composed of two different parts. Four self-contained scenes form the broad wooden edge and surround the slate top on which many single objects are strewn, some of which are done as trick pictures to look as if they were real. A round medallion with the alliance arms of Hans Baer, who commissioned the work (a brother-in-law of the burgomaster Jacob Meyer '⸏m hasen'), and his wife Barbara Brunner, adorns the centre. Two popular figures appear above and below the medallion: the 'Nobody' surrounded by broken objects, and the 'sleeping pedlar' whose basket is being unpacked by monkeys and the contents scattered around. St. Nobody, popularly regarded as the innocent guilty one, is sitting sadly with a lock on his mouth in the midst of broken china and as the saying above his head indicates is wailing: ,'Ich (bin der) Nieman / all Ding m(uss) ich verbrochen han / das t(rur)en ich / Das ich / nit kan verantworten mich' (I am the Nobody, who is blamed for everything; I am sad because I cannot defend myself). A humorous poem by Ulrich von Hutten, printed in Basle at that time, which gave a new version to the old popular figure of 'Nobody', must have inspired the scene (cf. *Kinkel, Mosaik zur Kunstgeschichte, Artikel 10,*

and *Heinrich Kohlhausen, Anzeiger, Germanisches National museum, 1936–39*).

The trick paintings done in thick impasto, a particularly fine achievement of the artist, lie scattered over the decorations of the table. They include a sealed letter with the seal nearby, on which is engraved a house sign and the initials 'H.H.', a pair of spectacles, a quill pen and paper knife, a playing card and other objects. On the long sides are many-figured tournament and hunting scenes, which show an excellent observation of life; on the small sides the painter depicts on the one fishing scenes and life by the water in a dry, humorous manner, on the other bird and girl catching. The painted table must have been commissioned during the first half of the year 1515, for Baer fought and died at Marignano on 13/14 September. Table painters were already known in Basle in the fifteenth century so that it can be assumed that the widespread fashion was still popular later and that this example, preserved by chance, was in no way anything unusual. The realistic genre like illustrational style and the technique of the painting were not only borrowed from the Elder Hans but were common to Late Gothic painting in Augsburg. The same characteristics appear in Thomas Burgkmair's 'Legend of St. Benedict', in the early works of Jörg Breu the Elder and in the works of Leonhard Beck. The present state of the painting, much darkened and badly scratched, is the result of the mishaps it has suffered. From Basle it came into the possession of the Berne painter Jacob Düntz, who, according to the donors' book, presented it to the Kunstkammer of the citizen's library at Zurich in 1633, where it was described as a 'table top, finely painted with various objects by the famous painter' (cf. *P. Ganz, Zürcher Kunstsinn und Kunstsammeln, Zürich, 1943*). Patin and Sandrart saw and described the table; during the eighteenth century it found its way to the basement of the Wasserkirche and was only discovered, badly scratched and damaged, amongst a lot of old lumber, in 1871 by Professor S. Vögelin, who published it with engraved reproductions, Vienna 1878.

As the table top, which has been twice restored, gives no uniform impression, an attempt was made to restore the unity in the photograph by retouching the scratched and rubbed-off parts—with the astonishing results seen in our reproduction (cf. *P. Ganz, Der Holbeintisch, Zeitschrift für Schweizerische Archäologie und Kunstgeschichte, 1950*, and the articles by *Ernst Buchner, Augsburger Kunst der Spätgotik und Renaissance, II, Beiträge zur Geschichte der deutschen Kunst, Augsburg, 1928*).

153–154. SIGNBOARD FOR A SCHOOLMASTER, PAINTED ON BOTH SIDES AND DATED 1516 ON EACH SIDE. Split apart later. Oil and tempera on pinewood. 1 ft. 10 in. × 2 ft. 2 in. *Basle, Öffentliche Kunstsammlung (Amerbach-Kabinett)*.
PLATE 196–197

The same ten-line text painted in Gothic minuscule letters encouraging people to learn to read and write in German, each explained by a genre-like scene, appears on both sides. One side represents a schoolroom; the schoolmaster is using a rod to teach a pupil to write whilst the schoolmistress opposite is teaching a girl; two more advanced pupils are sitting reading on the bench.

On the other side the schoolmaster is explaining to one young apprentice how to write; a second one, sitting on a chair opposite, holds a quill pen in his hand and has writing materials in front of him.

The schoolmaster portrayed by Holbein was certainly Oswald Molitor, known as Myconius, from Lucerne, who belonged to the circle of Froben and who owned the copy of Erasmus' 'Laus Stultitiae' adorned with marginal drawings by Holbein, which was illustrated in 1515/16. In addition to his studies he was a schoolmaster at Kleinbasle and at St. Peter, helped by his wife; later he went to the monastic school at Zurich and then to Lucerne and in 1531 he was elected 'Antistes' (Chief Warden) of the Basle church to replace Oecolampadius.

155. PRINTER'S EMBLEM OF JOHANNES FROBEN OF BASLE. 1523. Inscribed: IOAN FROB. Tempera on canvas, heightened with gold. 17½ × 12¾. *Basle, Öffentliche Kunstsammlung (Amerbach-Kabinett)*.   PLATE 199
The composition is based on St. Matthew, X, 16: 'Behold I send you forth as sheep in the midst of wolves be ye therefore wise as serpents, and harmless as doves', combined with the classical symbol of commerce, the wand of Mercury. A later hand has gone over it with a pen and framed it with a broad, black line. The signet appears for the first time in Froben's printing office in 1523 (*Heitz and Bernoulli, Basler Büchermarken, No. 46*). Froben's grandson, the printer Aurelius Erasmus Froben, presented this work of Holbein's—which is attributed to Ambros by *Woltman*, to Hans by *His*—to Basilius Amerbach in 1538 (cf. *P. Ganz, C.R. 462*).

156–157. INNER SIDES OF THE FOLDING DOORS OF THE ORGAN-CASE IN THE BASLE MINSTER, WITH FOUR MONUMENTAL FIGURES, THE BASLE MINSTER AND A CONCERT OF ANGELS. 1525/26. Oil and tempera on canvas, 9 ft. 3 in. × 14 ft. 10 in. *Basle, Öffentliche Kunstsammlung*.
PLATES 200–201 (202–203)

The organ-case, known to us from drawings by Emanuel Büchel (Fig. 35), was richly carved in the style of the Early Renaissance. The folding doors were decorated with scroll work on the outer sides and painted on the inner sides with the colossal figures of the Imperial donor pair Henry and Cunigunde, the Virgin Mary, patroness of the Bishopric and the first bishop Pantalus.

Holbein exploited brilliantly the area at his disposal and achieved the effectiveness of his representations, which appeared thirty-six feet above the ground, by mock spatial motives and a strongly foreshortened view. The four statues, sculptured in the round, fill the high, narrow areas and appear to project over the surface through the cross of the Empress, the elbow of Henry, the knee of the Virgin and the right leg of the infant Christ as well as the crook of the Bishop; the low spaces between the figures show on the left the minster seen from the East and on the right a group of angels praising the Virgin and making music. The brown colour makes the scenes appear like wood carving, thus adapting them to the organ-case.

It is without doubt due to their high position that these saints escaped the iconoclastic storms of 1529; in 1639 during a restoration of the organ they were overpainted by Sixt Ringlin and were given to the public library in 1786 together with part of the carving of the organ-case. In 1843 they entered the *Kunstsammlung* and there they were restored in 1909–11, when many overpaintings were removed.

The introduction of the Reformation in February 1528 makes it probable that the work was commissioned before 1526, when the Bishop and Chapter still resided at Basle. Stylistic criteria indicate the year 1523/24 for the sketch composed of six vertical bands now in the *Öffentliche Kunstsammlung* (*P. Ganz, C.R. 110*), whereas the finished painting, in its greater monumentality, belongs to the mature style of the artist, after his visit to France. Various authors, including *Davies* and *Chamberlain*, date the shutters as early as 1522 and 1525 respectively, whilst others, for instance *H. A. Schmid, Waetzoldt* and *Stein* do not put them before 1528 and think that they were commissioned by Bishop Philip von Gundelsheim, who was elected in 1527.

FIG. 35 (Cat. Nos. 156-157). THE ORGAN-CASE WITH THE WINGS PAINTED BY HOLBEIN IN THE BASLE MINSTER
After a water-colour by Emanuel Büchel, 1775

158–161. THE PAINTINGS ON THE FAÇADE OF THE HERTEN-STEIN HOUSE IN LUCERNE. 1517/18. PLATE 195

Except for a small fragment from the top row, these paintings have been entirely destroyed. The three-storeyed Gothic house with its high, pointed roof and two stone corbel gables, which was built for the magistrate Jacob of Hertenstein, stood at the corner of the 'Kapell' square and the 'Sterngasse'. It is illustrated with remnants of the paintings in the plan of the town engraved on copper by Martin Martini in 1596. When the house was pulled down in the spring of 1825, the paintings still distinguishable were copied at the insti-gation of Colonel May von Büren and Karl Pfyffer von Altishofen by a group of painters, thus making it possible to attempt a reconstruction of the façade painting as a whole.

The decoration consisted of two quite separate parts; three continuous pictorial friezes adorned the two upper floors, whilst the two lower ones with the main picture between the windows of the first floor formed a sham architectural setting. The top picture frieze between the windows immediately below the roof illustrated five scenes from ancient history which showed high ethical qualities. The treacherous schoolmaster of Falerii who was whipped back to the town from the enemy camp by his own pupils; Leaena before the judges; Mucius Scaevola before Porsenna; the death of Lucretia, and the death leap of Marcus Curtius. The space between the two upper rows of windows was adorned with a triumphal procession composed by Holbein from an etching of Mantegna which belonged to Hans Amerbach in Basle, whilst the fields between the lower windows showed the four alliance arms of the magistrate in an architectural setting like all the other scenes. A room projecting from the façade through its painted construction, with a cupola resting on columns, formed the transition to the

FIG. 36 (CAT. NO. 161). ORIGINAL DESIGN FOR 'LEAINA BEFORE THE JUDGES'
Basle, Öffentliche Kunstsammlung

purely sham architecture below, in which, probably for the benefit of the magistrate's sons, was related the legend of the three pretenders to the throne. In this the true heir is recognized because he refuses to shoot at his father's dead body. Of the decoration of the first floor and of the ground floor, only two Renaissance friezes with cherubs, above, and antique statues between the windows are known from hearsay but an original drawing by Holbein has been preserved which appears to be a design for the ornamentation of the entrance door and the lower windows of the entrance hall.

It can be seen from the copies that the pictorial frieze in the upper part of the façade corresponds in style to the dated works of 1516 and 1517 and so in any case originated before Holbein's journey to Italy, whereas the painting on the ground and first floors with their sham architecture in the style of the early Renaissance in Lombardy do not seem to have been done until after

Fig. 37 (Cat. Nos. 158-161). RECONSTRUCTION OF THE HERTENSTEIN HOUSE AT LUCERNE, WITH HOLBEIN'S FRESCOES

Fig. 38 (Cat. No. 159). RECONSTRUCTION OF THE HERTENSTEIN FRESCOES, by A. Landerer

Fig. 39 (Cat. No. 160). ORIGINAL DESIGN FOR AN ENTRANCE PORCH

his return. In any case the paintings on the lower part were enriched by Italian motives and were more mature in style (*P. Ganz, Holbeins Italienfahrt* in *Süddeutsche Monatshefte, 1909*). The lack of style in the watercolour copies, done before the house was pulled down, make it impossible for us to have more than a general idea of the content of the wall paintings which adorned two rooms on the second floor and two large rooms and a corner room on the third floor. They do, however, show that, like the table-top genre scenes of 1515, they were in the manner of Augburg historical painting and probably revealed the same type of humour. It is quite possible that this important commission was executed from Holbein's own designs but with the help of his father's workshop. His father and his father's brother Sigmund left Augsburg in 1517.

158. Reconstruction of the Hertenstein House with the frescoes by the architect Walter Spiess in *Basle*.
FIGURE 37–38
The main sources were Martin Martini's town plan of 1596, on which the frescoes are still indicated, and the reconstruction by A. Landerer after the watercolour copies in the Lucerne library (cf. *Joseph Schneller, Die Fresken des Hertensteinhauses* in *Geschichtsfreund, XXVIII, 1873;* and *Th. von Liebenau, Hans Holbein d. J. Fresken am Hertensteinhaus in Luzern, 1888*).

159. Collatinus, the Husband of Lucretia. Fragment from the 'Death of Lucretia'. Oil on dry ground. 4 ft. 5½ in. × 2 ft. 1½ in. *Lucerne, Museum.* PLATE 198.
The scene appeared between the two windows to the right of the central axis of the top floor and is the sole remnant of the whole façade painting.

160. Design for an Entrance Porch and a Vestibule Window, probably intended for the Hertenstein House (*P. Ganz, C.R. 112*). Pen and ink, partly heightened with red. *Basle, Print-room of the Öffentliche Kunstsammlung (Amerbach-Kabinett).* FIGURE 39

161. Leaena before the Judges. Original design for the second of the ancient history scenes on the top floor (*P. Ganz, C.R. 111*). Pen and Indian ink. *Print-room, Basle, Amerbach-Kabinett.* FIGURE 36
Leaena, the mistress of the tyrant slayer Aristogeiton, bit out her tongue to avoid the temptation of betraying her lover during the trial.

162–165. The Paintings on the two Façades of the 'House of the Dance' in the Eisengasse in Basle. 1520/22. The building was pulled down in 1909.
The three-storeyed corner house of the 'Dance', which can be traced back to 1401, belonged in Holbein's day to the wealthy goldsmith Balthasar Angelrot, a brother-in-law of the donor of the Solothurn altarpiece. The narrow main façade faced the principal street and had a doorway and casement windows with pointed arches on the ground floor. The side façade, facing the 'Helmgässlein',

was considerably larger and included two further houses adjacent to the 'Dance' house.
An original drawing by Holbein and various copies by the Basle painter Nicolas Rippel in 1590 (*KdK. 161, 162*) as well as other replicas have made it possible to form a general idea of the whole decoration. The corner which projected on to the Rheingasse leading to the Rhine gate was selected by Holbein for the central point of the whole composition. From here using a sham architecture he combined the asymmetrically arranged windows of the two house façades into a Renaissance structure.
The main façade of the house and the part of the side façade visible from the street formed a self-contained composition, to which the continuation of the painting towards the 'Helmgässlein' was attached by means of a large archway. The heavy pillars adorned with garlands on the ground floor supported a projecting cornice on both façades, on which pairs of peasants in wild abandon danced towards the corner of the house to the tune of bagpipes and oboes. Above them, between the windows of the first floor, antique statues stood against the walls similar to the Hertenstein House in Lucerne, but on the second floor, in place of the loggia, a balcony projected, supported by consols; on this balcony various inhabitants of the house and a dog were to be seen. The third floor showed on each façade a triumphal arch adorned with sculptures joined together by a high, pointed arch. Building still continued on the top floor, masonry tools lay around and a paint pot had been left behind; the blue sky was visible between the uncompleted brick walls. This genre-like solution is scarcely conceivable in Holbein's later monumental style of decoration. It belonged, like the genre-paintings on the walls facing the 'Helmgässlein', to the early period and showed among other things a stable lad next to a tied-up horse, a barrel with tippling Bacchanalian youths and a cat slinking off with a mouse between its teeth. The architectural motives and the figural sculpture were still under direct Lombard influence; their prototypes can be deduced from the monuments in Milan. Like the early glass designs, they were united in a decorative manner but not yet fully combined to form an architectural entity. Marcus Curtius, too, as he appeared above the doorway leaping into the chasm over the head of a soldier bending in front of him, showed the Milanese influence. Holbein must have seen one of the models or drawings by Leonardo for an equestrian statue of Ludovico il Moro or Marshall Trivulzio. The figures, placed in a not very imposing manner against the façade merely repeat Leonardo's group as they appear in the four-rider study at Windsor, without any personal artistic feeling (*Wilhelm Suida, Leonardo und sein Kreis, 1929, fig. 72*). It follows from all this that the two house façades cannot have been executed after his first stay in England.
For this extensive work Holbein received 40 gulders. The House of the Dance was the only one of his house paintings that Holbein approved of when he saw them again on a visit to Basle during a business trip in 1538.

Fig. 40 (Cat. No. 162). RECONSTRUCTION OF THE 'HOUSE OF THE DANCE', formerly in the Eisengasse in Basle, with Holbein's frescoes

FIG. 41 (Cat. No. 163) DESIGN FOR THE DECORATION OF THE FAÇADE ON THE EISENGASSE

F<small>IG</small>. 42 (Cat. No. 164). D<small>ESIGN FOR THE DECORATION OF THE FAÇADE ON THE HELMGAESSLEIN</small>

According to a record made by Amerbach's son-in-law he described them as 'ein wenig gut' (quite good).

Patin was still able to see the paintings in 1676 and Müller mentions them for the last time as in a 'thoroughly defective condition', in his book *Merkwurdige Überbleibsel von Alterthümern*, published in Zurich in 1777.

162. RECONSTRUCTION OF THE 'HOUSE OF THE DANCE' WITH THE FRESCOES by the architect Walter Spiess in Basle. *Basle, Historisches Museum.* FIGURE 40

Based on Merian's town plan of 1615 and H. E. v Berlepschs fresco-reconstruction of 1878 made from the original drawing and old copies (*KdK. 159*).

163. DESIGN FOR THE HOUSE FAÇADE IN THE EISENGASSE (*P. Ganz, C.R. 113*). Pen and watercolour. *Berlin, Print-room.* FIGURE 41

The big sheet seems to be an enlarged workshop drawing of the final version. The *Öffentliche Kunstsammlung* in Basle possesses a variant, partly executed in pen and ink, of the architecture in the upper part of the façade (*P. Ganz, C.R. 114*). The date 1520 appears on a sixteenth-century copy, also in Basle, which agrees with my view that the decorations for the 'House of the Dance' preceded the ones for the town hall.

164. DESIGN FOR THE FAÇADE facing the HELMGÄSSLEIN. Copy. Pen and watercolour. *England, unknown Private Collection.* FIGURE 42

One part with the equestrian figure of Marcus Curtius and the Roman soldier standing below him was copied by Nicolas Rippel in 1590 with the remark: 'in frontis-picie domus (at the gable side of the house) (illustrated *KdK. 161*).

165. THE PEASANT DANCE, THE REAL EMBLEM OF THE HOUSE. Watercolour copy by Nicolas Rippel in 1623. *Basle, Öffentliche Kunstsammlung.* FIGURE 43–44

Holbein also drew this subject, which he had borrowed from Dürer, for a woodcut as the lower border for book-titles (W. 232, 233). As in Dürer's engraving (B. 90), the wildness of the dance is particularly emphasized. Several old copies exist in pen and ink and wash and in water-colour as well as reproductions in oil, the best proof of the fame of the composition.

FIGS. 43-44 (Cat. No. 165). THE PEASANT DANCE. Watercolour copies

FIG. 45 (Cat. No. 166). ORIGINAL DESIGN FOR THE DECORATION OF A HOUSE FAÇADE

166. DESIGN FOR THE UPPER PART OF A HOUSE FAÇADE, probably for the Amerbach house *Zum Kaiserstuhl* in the Rheingasse in Kleinbasle. 1524 (*P. Ganz, C.R. 115*). *Pen drawing. Basle, Print-room of the Öffentliche Kunstsammlung (Amerbach-Kabinett).* FIGURE 45

The picture with the enthroned emperor and the inscription tablet behind indicates that, like the 'Dance', this figure represented the self-evident house sign; it was only natural that the Amerbachs should get Holbein to decorate their house which was named *Zum Kaiserstuhl*. This house may be the second example of a painted house by Holbein mentioned by Sandrart in his *Deutsche Akademie* II, 1926 edition, p. 322).

167–174. THE WALL PAINTINGS IN THE GREAT COUNCIL CHAMBER OF THE BASLE TOWN HALL. 1521–1530.

Eleven fragments of three paintings have been preserved. Oil on dry ground. *Basle, Öffentliche Kunstsammlung.*

PLATES 204–213

The young artist owed the commission to decorate the Great Council Chamber, which was built between 1517 and 1521, and also his work for the Hertenstein House in Lucerne and the 'House of the Dance' in Basle, to the influence of his patron, the burgomaster Jacob Meyer 'zum hasen'. The chamber was on the upper floor of the back part of the building over the council room and was accessible from the court by a flight of stairs and from the back by the tower staircase. It was in the shape of an irregular square and had three windowless walls suitable for painting but with an unfavourable lighting from the window wall.

Holbein painted a Renaissance order of columns on the

wall-space above the council seats placed round the walls, which permitted a view into the open, and niches in which painted statues were placed to enhance the plastic effect of the decoration. The selection of the scenes is supposed to have been made by the humanist Beatus Rhenanus, a friend of Erasmus, who lived at Basle; the scenes from the Old Testament and from ancient history were intended to serve as a perpetual warning to the councillors to do their duty and to be just. The series of pictures in half-life size began in the south-west corner of the room over the mayor's chair and showed Justice with the sword in her right hand standing on a balcony pointing to an inscription tablet on which was written 'O VOS REIGENTES OBLITI PRIVATORVM PVBLICA CVRATE' (O ye rulers, forget your private ends and serve the common weal). This was followed, immediately to the right, by kings Croesus and Sapor, the law-givers Charondas and Zaleucus, Curius Dentatus, king Rehoboam and Samuel meeting Saul; in between were single figures in niches with scroll bands: Justice, Wisdom, Temperance, David, Christ, Anacharsis, Harpocrates and Hezekiah Owing to Meyer's dismissal from office and to the changed political conditions the work was broken off in 1522-3 after Holbein in ten months' work had completed two thirds of the room, i.e. two walls.

The painting of the narrow Eastern wall was only done after Holbein's return from England and the choice of subject-matter was adapted to the new religious ideas. The two wall paintings were separated and framed by free standing candelabra pillars and in their clarity of composition and vivid presentation they showed the mature style of Holbein's art. They were executed during the four months from June to September in 1530.

Most of the compositions are preserved in three original drawings by Holbein, eight contemporary workshop copies, pen drawings and watercolour copies made by Jerome Hess of Basle in 1817, on the occasion of the re-discovery of certain of the wall paintings. They are all in the Print-room of the *Öffentliche Kunstsammlung* in Basle; only Croesus, Anacharsis, Harpocrates and King Hezekiah are missing.

The wall paintings, which Holbein wished to re-paint when he saw them during his visit in 1538, because he no longer liked them, were restored and patched up by Hans Bock but later allowed to fall into decay.

For the frescoes in the town hall cf. *H. A. Schmid, Die Werke Hans Holbeins in Basel, Öffentliche Kunstsammlung, small guide 2*, and *Rudolf Riggenbach, Der Grossratssaal und die Wandbilder Hans Holbeins d. J.*, in *Die Kunstdenkmäler des Kantons Basel-Stadt, I, Basle, 1932, p. 530-608*.

167. JUSTICE WARNS THE COUNCIL. Copy after an original Design (*P. Ganz, C.R. c.11*)   FIGURE 46
The motive of the figure behind the balustrade was also to be seen on the 'House of the Dance'.

FIG. 46 (Cat. No. 167). JUSTICE. Copy of the original design

168. KING SAPOR OF PERSIA HUMILIATES THE ROMAN EMPEROR VALERIAN. Original sketch by Holbein in pen and ink, tinted with watercolour (*P. Ganz, C.R. 116*).
FIGURE 47
The scene takes place in front of the Basle town hall. On either side of the historical scene the allegorical figures of Wisdom and Temperance appear in niches (*P. Ganz, C.R. 1, c10 and c12*).

169. CHARONDAS, THE LAW-GIVER OF TIRYNS, TAKES HIS OWN LIFE.   PLATES 204–205; FIGURE 48
A copy of the original sketch (*P. Ganz, C.R. c7*) and two heavily overpainted fragments have been preserved, (*a*) the head of Charondas 13 × 7½, (*b*) the head of a terrified onlooker 9 × 7.
Breaking the law he had himself made, Charondas entered the council meeting armed and took his own life to uphold the law.
The two fragments and the copy done by Jerome Hess in 1817 show that Holbein altered the composition when he did the wall painting. According to Hess' reproduction it was dated 1521 on the front left pilaster. King David appeared in a niche between this and the following painting (*P. Ganz, C.R. c8*).

FIG. 47 (Cat. No. 168). WISDOM: copy of the original design; KING SAPOR HUMILIATING THE EMPEROR VALERIAN: original design; TEMPERANCE: copy of the original design

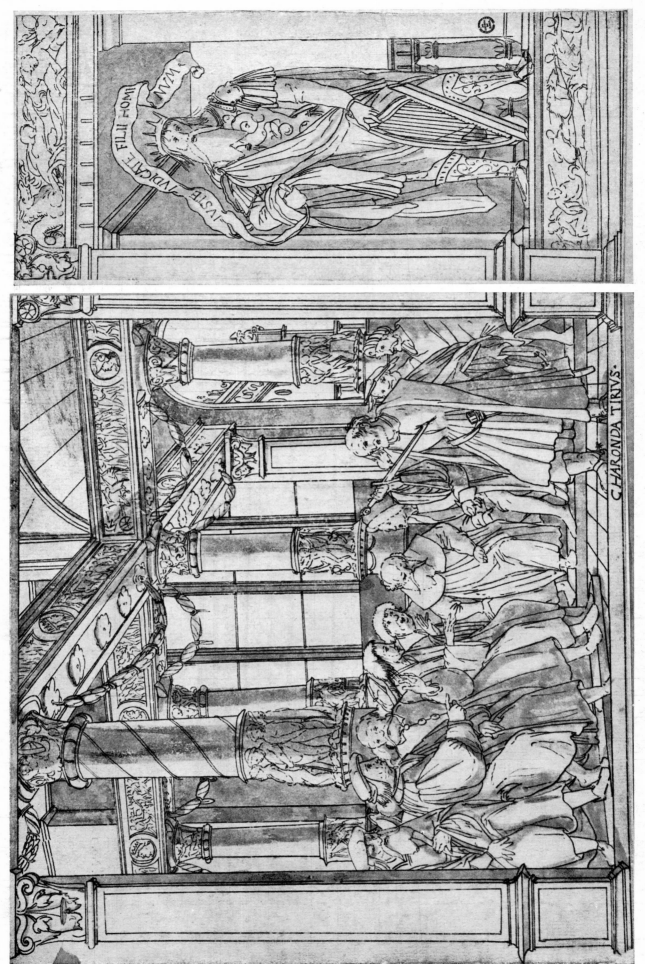

Fig. 48 (Cat. No. 169). CHARONDAS TAKING HIS OWN LIFE; KING DAVID. Copies of the original designs

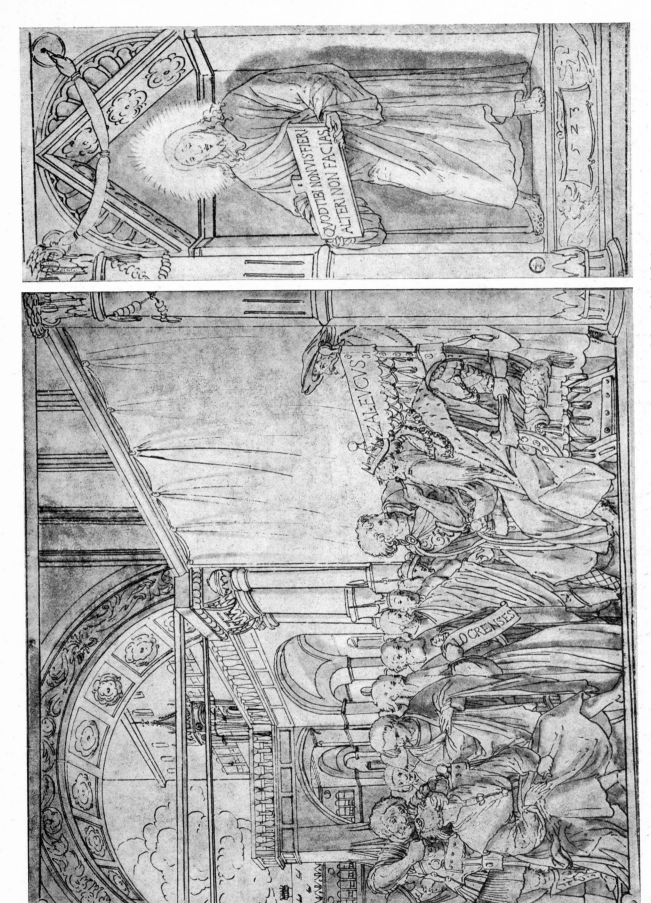

FIG. 49 (Cat. No. 170). THE BLINDING OF ZALEUCUS; CHRIST. Copies of the original designs

170. THE BLINDING OF ZALEUCUS OF LOCRI. Copy of an original sketch (*P. Ganz, C.R. c6*) which Holbein executed without any change. This is confirmed by copies made in 1559 and 1817. A common perspective unites this composition with the previous one. Christ in a niche stands at the side of Zaleucus and holds out a scroll band to the councillors. The translation of the Latin inscription is as follows: 'What thou wouldst not to thyself have done, that in thy turn do to no one' (Fig. 49). Beneath the figure is the date 1523.

171. THE SAMNITE AMBASSADORS BEFORE THE ROMAN CONSUL MARCUS CURIUS DENTATUS. Preserved in a watercolour copy made by Jerome Hess in 1817 and also a fragment of the original painting with the heads of the Samnite Ambassadors. 1522. $19\frac{5}{8} \times 19\frac{1}{2}$.

PLATE 206 (FIGURE 50)

As opposed to the wall surface painted so far, the wall between the passage to the waiting room and the entrance from the tower staircase formed an upright area so that in order to maintain the continuity of the horizontal line the historical scenes had to be continued in the upper half. This gave the artist the opportunity to paint the council messenger in life-size as he mounts the steps and touches his hat in greeting at the sight of the assembled council. This original idea in no way disturbed the sense of the scene above it but on the contrary brought it more up to date.

Marcus Curius Dentatus was regarded as the prototype of Roman incorruptibility; he was depicted rejecting the gold presents of the Samnites, intended as a condemnation of the custom, also prevalent in Basle at that time, of accepting foreign pensions.

The inscriptions and positions only are known of the niche figures; above the stove Anacharsis, over the passage to the waiting room Harpocrates, the god of silence, and King Hezekiah.

172. THE ANGER OF REHOBOAM. Original sketch preserved in pen and watercolour (*P. Ganz, C.R. 117*) and seven fresco fragments: King Rehoboam threatening the judges (joined together and completed).

PLATES 207–213 (FIGURE 51)

Heads of Councillors	$11\frac{3}{8} \times 11\frac{3}{8}$
Group of three men	$11\frac{3}{8} \times 9\frac{1}{2}$
Head of an old man	$6\frac{7}{8} \times 5\frac{7}{8}$
Heads of two spectators, half back view	$6\frac{1}{8} \times 5\frac{3}{8}$
Upper part of a bearded man	$3\frac{5}{8} \times 3$
Upper part of a the figures of a youth and a bearded man seen half-back view	$3\frac{1}{4} \times 4$

Before his election as king at Shechem, Rehoboam asked his father's old councillors and the companions of his own youth how he should treat the people. He followed the advice of the latter who recommended harshness not mildness as did the former (I Kings, 12).

In the distance on the right is the coronation of Jeroboam, the future king of Israel.

The finished work shows marked alterations from the sketch; the king, threatening with the little finger of his left hand, is no longer in full face but in profile, probably to emphasize the movement of his arm, and this made a regrouping of the councillors necessary. Some of the old councillors and young friends of the king are exceptionally well characterized.

173. THE PROPHET SAMUEL CURSES THE VICTORIOUS KING SAUL. Original sketch in pen and watercolours (*P. Ganz, C.R. 128*). FIGURE 52

At Jehovah's command Saul conquered the Amalekites under their King Agag but did not destroy the whole people as he had been enjoined to do and for that reason he was dethroned by Samuel (I Samuel, 15). The fresco was copied on canvas in 1579 by Hans Bock.

174. CHRIST AND THE WOMAN TAKEN IN ADULTERY. Copy of the original sketch (*P. Ganz, C.R. 53*). FIGURE 53

This composition, which was probably destined for the decoration of the third wall, was never executed.

In 1579 Hans Jakob Pläpp used the scene for the central part of a glass window with the coats-of-arms of two Basle families.

175–176. THE GROUP PORTRAIT OF THOMAS MORE AND HIS FAMILY. 1527. The original pen sketch and seven preliminary studies for heads in black and coloured chalks have been preserved (*P. Ganz, C.R. 25–31; Parker, W.Dr. 1, 3–8*) also a painted study for the portrait of Lady More and several copies (*Catalogue No. 42* above).

The portrait, probably commissioned on the occasion of the scholar's fiftieth birthday, shows him surrounded by his large family. It is the first example of an intimate group portrait not of devotional or ceremonial character to be painted this side of the Alps. At that time Thomas More was living in his country house in Chelsea with his second wife Alice, his father, his only son and his son's fiancée, three married daughters, eleven grandchildren and a relative Margaret Giggs. The artist, who had been recommended to him by his friend Erasmus, was also enjoying his hospitality. The original is lost; if, as I assume, it was executed as a wall painting in the same technique as the Basle town hall paintings, then it perished or was destroyed on the spot, after More's property had been confiscated by the king. If painted on canvas like the decorations for the banqueting hall of the Hanseatic merchants of the London Steelyard, then it may perhaps only have disappeared. In any case it adorned one of the rooms in the newly built part of the country house in Chelsea, probably the library, which was finished in 1523, or the dining room. There are no valid reasons for the assumption that Holbein left his work unfinished and that it was completed by another artist.

The final version of the group portrait, which Holbein began as early as February 1527 and must have completed before his return to Basle, has been handed down

FIG. 50 (Cat. No. 171). THE SAMNITE AMBASSADORS BEFORE THE ROMAN CONSUL. Copy by H. Hess
after the destroyed fresco

FIG. 51 (Cat. No. 172). ORIGINAL DESIGN FOR THE 'ANGER OF REHOBOAM'

Fig. 52 (Cat. No. 173). Original Design for 'Samuel and Saul'

FIG. 53 (Cat. No. 174). CHRIST AND THE WOMAN TAKEN IN ADULTERY. Copy of the original design

in various copies of the same size, the oldest of which is dated 1530. Three of the copies were in the possession of three of Sir Thomas More's children or their heirs. A fourth copy, possibly intended for the fourth child Elizabeth Dancy, is mentioned by Carel van Mander's informant in 1604 in the collection of the art amateur Andries de Loo in London. Later this copy was in the Arundel Collection and in 1661 belonged to the brothers von Imstenraedt in Cologne. It finally reached Vienna, where it was auctioned in 1670 (cf. *Koegler, p. 88* and *O. Kurz, Bur- lington Magazine, 1943, p. 279 ff.*).

175. COPY OF THE GROUP PORTRAIT by Richard Locky. Inscribed and dated: Richardus Locky Fec. ano 1530. Oil on canvas. 8 ft. 2 in. × 13 ft. 1 in. *Nostell Priory, Lord St. Oswald.*   FIGURE 56 (54)

The copy from Well Hall in Kent, the seat of the Roper family, was inherited by the Winn family and is today at Nostell Priory. It was probably commissioned by Sir Thomas More for his favourite daughter Margaret

Roper (cf. *Maurice W. Brockwell, Catalogue of the Pictures and other Works of Art at Nostell Priory, London, 1915, pp. 79-98*). The picture which has been considerably altered from the sketch, shows the composition in its final version and reveals the efforts of the copyist to follow Holbein's model down to the last detail; the dry execution shows the same hand throughout which, in my opinion, precludes the possibility, suggested by *Chamberlain* and *H. A. Schmid*, that Locky completed an unfinished work by Holbein.

A second copy at East Hendred, which has been cut down by the removal of the portrait of Lady More on the right, was originally at Barnborough near Doncaster, the seat of the Cresacre family, where John More, the only son of the Lord Chancellor, had moved after the death of his father-in-law Cresacre. The third copy which, like the second, seems to have been copied from the version at Nostell Priory, was reported to have belonged to Giles Heron of Heron Hall, Essex, the husband of Cecily More. Through inheritance it passed to the Tyrells at

FIG. 54 (Cat. No. 175). CECILY HERON AND MARGARET ROPER. Detail from the group portrait (Fig. 56)

Heron from there to the collection of Lord Petre at Thorndon near Brentford.

In 1593 Thomas More, the son of John and grandson of the Lord Chancellor, had a new group portrait painted with eleven life-sized figures which is described and illustrated in the catalogue of the collection of Lord Lee of Fareham (cf. *KdK. 193* and *Tancred Borenius, A Catalogue of the Pictures etc. at 18 Kensington Palace Gardens 1923, collected by Viscount and Viscountess Lee of Fareham*). It consists: (*1*) of a copy of the old group portrait, minus the portrait of Lady More, the step-grandmother, the relative Margaret Giggs and the jester Patersen and (*2*) of Thomas More with his wife and two sons added on the

right with a portrait of Anne Cresacre his mother as an old woman hanging on the wall above him. Various copies were also made of this group portrait.

176. SKETCH FOR THE GROUP PORTRAIT OF SIR THOMAS MORE AND HIS FAMILY (*P. Ganz, C.R. 24*). Original pen drawing on white paper. *Basle, Öffentliche Kunstsammlung (Amerbach-Kabinett).*   FIGURE 55

In this pen sketch Holbein has arranged the family in two groups according to their importance, probably following More's instructions. Sir Thomas More, the head of the family, occupies the central place in the whole composition. On his right is his father, who sits

FIG. 55 (Cat. No. 176). ORIGINAL DESIGN FOR THE MORE FAMILY GROUP. 1527

K

Fig. 56 (Cat. No. 175). GROUP PORTRAIT OF THOMAS MORE AND HIS FAMILY, 1527–8. Copy by R. Locky. 1530. Nostell Priory, Lord St. Oswald

in the centre of the diagonally placed group, on his left his son. In the small group kneeling in the foreground, Margaret Roper, More's favourite daughter, dominates whilst his second wife Alice Middleton, separated by the prie-dieu, rounds off the picture. Alterations drawn in and notes referring to them in Holbein's hand reveal that the design had been carefully discussed, for they have been followed in part in the finished version.

More sent the drawing with Holbein to Erasmus at Basle so as to introduce his family to him, for which purpose the names and ages were added, according to recent research, by Nicolas Kratzer, who taught astronomy to More's daughters (cf. *Otto Pächt* in *Burlington Magazine*, *1944/5, p. 138*).

In two letters to Sir Thomas and Margaret Roper, dated Sept. 5/6, 1529, Erasmus sent his enthusiastic thanks: 'I cannot put into words the deep pleasure I felt when the painter Holbein gave me the picture of your whole family which is so completely successful that I should scarcely be able to see you better if I were with you.' (Printed in the original Latin by *P. S. and H. M. Allen, Opus epistolorum Des. Erasmi, vol. 8, Nos. 2211, 2212.*) The brilliant characterization in the drawing of each individual is, even today, among the most outstanding achievements of Holbein's art (cf. *P. Ganz, Zwei Werke Hans Holbeins d. J. aus der Frühzeit des ersten englischen Aufenthaltes* in *Festschrift zur Eröffnung des Kunstmuseums in Basle, 1936; Doris Wild, Holbein and Leonardo, Anzeiger für Schweizerische Altertumskunde, 1936/I*). *H. A. Schmid* regards it as a copy after the picture.

177–178. THE WALL PAINTINGS IN THE BANQUETING HALL OF THE GUILDHALL OF THE STEELYARD IN LONDON: Triumphal Processions of Riches and Poverty. 1532/33. The originals, which have disappeared, were painted in grisaille on a blue background heightened with gold and lightly tinted in watercolour on canvas. Preserved only in an original sketch and copies.

The content of the two wall paintings corresponded to the motto of the Hanseatic merchants, which appeared in Latin over the main entrance to the colony and read in English: 'Gold is the father of joy and the son of care; he who lacks it is sad, he who has it is uneasy.' As in the Basle town hall paintings the program was no doubt decided in detail by the patrons who commissioned the work. It was composed by Holbein after popular Italian representations of symbolic triumphal processions. *Koegler* has found two literary sources, a comedy by Aristophanes, and Lucian's Dialogue 'Timon the Misanthropist', in which is related the quarrel between Plutus, the god of riches and Penia, the personification of poverty; they contain a number of figures that Holbein used in his painting (cf. *H. Koegler, Holbeins Triumphzüge des Reichtums und der Armut* in *Jahresbericht der Öffentlichen Kunstsammlung in Basel, 1931–32, p. 57 ff.*).

Like the Basel town hall, the wall with the window allowed no space for painting and this obviously dictated the arrangement of the two scenes. The brilliant procession of riches decorated the long wall of the hall and on the narrow wall, probably facing the entrance, was the condensed procession of poverty only half as long. I still maintain the suggestion I put forward years ago, namely that the 'Procession of Poverty' preceded that of 'Riches' because in this order the content is clearer and corresponds accurately to the above mentioned motto.

The two original paintings remained in the Steelyard when Queen Elizabeth dissolved the Hanseatic guild in 1589. When twenty years later James I returned their property to the Hanseatic merchants and the halls were let, the representatives of the German towns presented the two paintings, which had suffered heavily in the meantime, to Henry, Prince of Wales, the king's son. After the latter's early death they came into the collection of King Charles I and then, possibly through exchange, to that of the Earl of Arundel. There they were seen by Carel van Mander in 1627 and there Matthäus Merian the Younger drew the copy of the 'Procession of Poverty' in 1640, which is still preserved today (British Museum). With the Arundel Collection the paintings came to Amsterdam; they are listed in the inventory made in 1655 after the death of the countess of Arundel (cf. *Mary S. F. Hervey, p. 481*). Félibien's suggestion that the pictures passed from Flanders to Paris is unconfirmed, but *Otto Kurz (Burlington Magazine, 1943, p. 279 ff.*) has shown that in 1661 they belonged to the brothers Franz and Bernhard von Imstenraedt, two nephews of the famous collector Everard Jabach at Cologne, for at that time Franz, in bombastic Latin verse, offered them with his whole collection to the emperor Leopold for sale. Although the emperor refused the offer, the collection did come to Vienna where the two paintings and the group portrait of Sir Thomas More were auctioned on 21st April, 1670 and fell to the Cardinal Count Carl von Lichtenstein, bishop of Olmütz and Kremsier. In the inventory of the bishop's collection of paintings made in 1691, both pictures are listed as being in the upper gallery of the residence at Olmütz. No. 28 is described as the 'Triumph of Vanity, a large piece in an old gilt frame by Holbein, 1 piece' and No. 29 'Triumph of Poverty in gilt frame by Holbein, 1 piece'. Together with his entire property they were left by the bishop to his successor in office. Their further fate is not known. *Theodor von Frimmel*, who published the catalogue of the Vienna auction in 1909 in his *Blätter für Gemäldekunde*, pointed out that in 1752 there had been a fire at the bishop's palace in Kremsier in which part of the collection of pictures, probably including the Holbeins, had been destroyed. If these paintings really were the original ones, then we know their size from the entry in the Vienna catalogue. The 'Triumphal Procession of Riches' was, according to this, 20 ft. 3 in. long and 8 ft. high; that of Poverty, 9 ft. 10½ in. × 7 ft. 3½ in. They were therefore slightly under life-size (*Koegler, p. 85*).

An exact description of both paintings is given by Joachim von Sandrart in his *Academie der Bau- Bild- und Mahlerey-Künste* of 1675 (ed. *A. R. Peltzer, Munich, 1925,*

FIG. 57 (Cat. No. 177). ORIGINAL DESIGN FOR THE 'TRIUMPH OF RICHES'. Paris, Louvre

p, 101), but he made use of the description published by Carel van Mander. He had seen the originals in 1627 at the Arundel House in London; he also seems to have possessed the copies made by Federico Zuccaro in 1574 from the originals, or at any rate copies of these, which were later in the collection of Crozat in Paris and became the property of the Hesse-Darmstadt privy councillor Georg Wilhelm Fleischmann. Christian von Mechel used them as models for the etchings in his publication *Œuvre de Jean Holbein, Basle, 1780.*

The only coloured copies from the originals, with flesh-coloured heads, arms and legs, green trees and blue background are attributed to Lucas Vorsterman the Elder, who worked for the Earl of Arundel in 1642 and, according to Vertue, engraved both processions (cf. *H. Hymans, Lucas Vorsterman, Catalogue Raisonné de son œuvre, Brussels 1893,* where the only engraving preserved of the Triumph of Poverty, $25\frac{1}{4} \times 18\frac{3}{4}$, is mentioned as No. 108). Both were published by Waagen after the outline drawings of George Scharf in *Kugler's 'Handbook of Painting' 1860.* Once the property of Horace Walpole, they passed from his collection to that of Eastlake and J. P. Richter; the 'Triumph of Poverty' has been in the British Museum since 1894, the pendant remained in private hands. The best of the copies known today are the ones by Jan de Bisschop in the British Museum.

177. THE TRIUMPH OF RICHES. Original sketch in pen and Indian ink, heightened with body white. *Paris, Louvre (P. Ganz, C.R. 121),* also copy by Jan de Bisschop (about 1670) *London, British Museum.*   FIGURES 57–58

The procession is moving from right to left. The four horses, led by four allegorical women, Liberality, Good Faith, Equality and Justice, draw the Renaissance state coach driven by Reason, with Fortune seated inside holding the sail of luck and strewing money around her, whilst Plutus the God of riches is enthroned beneath a baldachin. Rich men from the ancient world stride along in pairs, followed by a group of riders with royal personages amongst whom Croesus and Cleopatra, according to Walpole, were supposed to represent Henry VIII and Anne Boleyn. Nemesis is hovering over the last group. In the background, left, is a tree.

The sketch contains 23 inscribed figures and a group of uninscribed ones at the end of the procession; a pen and ink copy in the British Museum and Borgiani's etching of 1561 reproduce them all accurately except that Cleopatra wears a crown and on the etching the kings have been increased by two and the names changed (cf. *Lawrence Binyon, Catalogue of drawings by British Artists and Artists of Foreign Origin working in Great Britain, British Museum, 1900, III, p. 342/343).*

Another version with 34 figures, which must have been taken from the original painting has been most completely represented in the copy attributed to Jan de Bisschop and retains in the main the same arrangement. It shows an increase in the number of representatives of riches, who now also accompany the procession at the back and a finer decoration of the coach in the form of a shell.

Seeing that the two pairs of heads, which appear next to the horses on Bisschop's copy, without names, are additions by the copyist, the number of persons is reduced to thirty. The main difference between original and copy, however, is in the attitude of Justice, who is looking backwards, and of Sichaeus, who is turning towards the spectator (cf. *Arthur M. Hind, Catalogue of Drawings by Dutch and Flemish Artists in the British Museum, 1926, III, p. 38/39).* Bisschop drew the two triumphal processions in Amsterdam when the Arundel Collection was there.

Since only 29 figures are to be seen in Federigo Zuccaro's older copy (Ill. *Koegler, p. 57*)—Heliogabalus and the nameless heads are missing—and that we know from the statements of the painter Goltzius and the inscription

FIG. 58 (Cat. No. 177). THE TRIUMPH OF RICHES. Copy by Jan de Bisschop. London, British Museum

FIG. 59 (Cat. No. 178). THE TRIUMPH OF POVERTY. Copy by Jan de Bisschop. London, British Museum

on the copy itself that Zuccaro's replica was made from the originals, it can safely be assumed that these were already badly damaged at that time and that certain details as well as the inscriptions, in part wrongly deciphered, were hard to read.

The facts that the catalogue of the Vienna auction gives the number of persons as 30 and not 23, and that the copies by Zuccaro were done from the paintings, make it probable that the composition with the additional figures was the one executed and that Holbein's original sketch represented a first version.

178. THE TRIUMPH OF POVERTY. Copy by Jan de Bisschop (about 1670). *London, British Museum.* FIGURE 59 Poverty, an old woman in rags, is sitting under a straw

roof in a cart which is being drawn by two donkeys (Stupidity and Ignorance) and two oxen (Indolence and Carelessness); Hope is driving the vehicle and behind her sit Industry, Profit, and Memory whilst at the back of the cart Misfortune is hitting the crowd of beggars at the tail end of the procession. At the head marches Diligence, who, with Modesty and Solicitude, is leading the vehicle; the central group behind Labour, a powerfully built woman, consists of workers to whom Industry is handing down tools. In addition to the above copies and the ones already mentioned by Zuccaro and Lucas Vorsterman, the British Museum has another one by Mathäus Merian the Younger dated 1640. The composition is the same throughout and there are 19 figures which tallies with the Vienna catalogue.

FIG. 60 (Cat. No. 179). THE FRESCO FORMERLY IN THE PRIVY CHAMBER AT WHITEHALL. Copy by Leemput, 1667

179. KING HENRY VIII, HIS FATHER KING HENRY VII AND THEIR WIVES. Wall painting formerly in the Privy Chamber of the palace at Whitehall, London. 1537. A small oil copy by Remi van Leemput (1667) has been preserved at Hampton Court Palace and the original cartoon for the figure group on the left; ink and wash and brush drawing lightly touched with watercolour (*P. Ganz, C.R. 122*). 8 ft. 5½ in. × 4 ft. 6 in. *Chatsworth, Duke of Devonshire.*

PLATE 214 (215–216) (FIGURE 60)

The original, decorating a wall without doors or windows, was destroyed when the palace was burnt down in 1698. The copy, made by the painter van Leemput in 1667 at the order of Charles II, and etched by Vertue (*KdK. 179*), is the only one that reproduces the whole picture; it shows the royal couple and the parents of Henry VIII in life-size on either side of a marble monument, on which are inscribed in Latin verse the virtues of both kings. In

FIG. 61 (Cat. No. 179). KING HENRY VIII. Copy of the fresco of 1537

front stand Henry VIII with his legs astride and his third wife Jane Seymour, with a pet dog at her feet; behind them, one step higher, stand Henry VII with his left arm resting on a cushion and Elizabeth of York. The background consists of a richly ornamented and sculptured Renaissance room, the central structure of which is an accurate copy of Bramante's large architectonic etching, as is apparently also the monument. Above the shell-shaped, vaulted niche at the side is a plastic frieze with inscription tablets held by tritons and sirens. They bear the initials H and J (Henry and Jane) entwined in a lover's knot on the left and the date 1537 on the right. On the painting, as opposed to the cartoon, Henry VIII was given in front view and instead of the white dress in which Holbein portrayed him in 1536, he wore a magnificent red and gold embroidered robe; this is also to be seen in later portraits.

As early as 1590 the cartoon was described in the catalogue of the art collection of John Lumley of Lumley Castle. Later it came into the possession of the Duke of Devonshire and was for a long time at Hardwick Hall (cf. *Illustrated Catalogue of Early English Portraiture, 1909, No. 40, p. 88/89*).

This full-length portrait of Henry VIII was copied many times during his lifetime and the execution and artistic quality of the wall painting is better rendered in the contemporary replicas than in the copy by Van Leemput. Such copies belong to the Duke of Rutland at Belvoir Castle (Fig. 61), to the Duke of Devonshire at Chatsworth, to the Seymour family, to whom the King himself is said to have given the picture as a present, and to the Walker Art Gallery, Liverpool.

From Samuel Pepys' *Diary*, in which on the occasion of a visit to Whitehall on August 28th 1628 he notes with regret that Holbein's ceiling paintings have been covered with whitewash, it would appear possible that Holbein painted the ceiling not only of the matted gallery, to which Pepys' entry has always been presumed to refer, but also of the Privy Chamber.

180. SOLOMON RECEIVES THE QUEEN OF SHEBA. This was in all likelihood the design for a lost wall painting at Whitehall. About 1537–40. Silverpoint, pen and brush, washed in colour heightened with gold. Vellum 9 × 7⅛. *Windsor Castle, H.M. The King (P. Ganz, C.R. 129 and Parker, W.Dr. Frontispiece).*

According to Fischart of Strassburg, who wrote a description of London in 1576, and Pepys (1668) various rooms at Whitehall, including the matted gallery, were decorated with paintings on walls and ceilings, some of which were attributed to Holbein. The scene is amongst the most beautiful and multi-figured examples of the artist's work. Here his feeling for beauty and harmony of composition find their most perfect expression. Here, too, one of the main problems of his art, how to portray a procession of men surging forwards, that had occupied him since his Christ carrying the Cross of 1515, finds its fullest and final solution in the alternating movement of the procession and in the lively gestures of figures and groups. The ceremonial scene is a flattery for the king; Solomon's features are those of Henry VIII, to whom the work, executed on vellum in the style of a miniature painting, was in all probability offered as a New Year present.

Numerous inscriptions explain the sense of the action and describe the 34 people represented; the scene is based on II Chronicles, ix, 5–8.

The painting in grisaille on a blue ground, in lightly coloured wash heightened with gold and white, corresponds to the execution of the wall paintings for the Guildhall of the Steelyard in London. This miniature picture was formerly in the Arundel Collection and was etched there by Wenzel Hollar.

181. King Henry VIII presents the Charter to the Barber-Surgeons' Guild in London. 1543. Unfinished. Oil and tempera on oak. 5 ft. 11 in. × 10 ft. 3 in. *London, Barbers' Hall, Monkwell Street.*   Plates 218–220

The painting was commissioned to celebrate the ceremonial presentation act of 1541. It depicts the conferment of the charter, which the president, kneeling as are all those in the front row, receives from the king. Henry VIII is represented larger than the members of the guild; he is sitting on a raised throne, behind which hangs a costly tapestry on the wall. To the right kneel the three physicians of the king (fig. 35), two of whom, Chambers and Butts, were also portrayed by Holbein in single portraits; to the left the president and seven other members of the guild.

Originally there was a double window above this group with a view of the old steeple of St. Bride's which indicates that the ceremony took place not in Whitehall but in the old Bridewell Palace. The row of portraits beneath the window was added during the sixteenth century. In this state the painting described by Carel van Mander in 1604, was copied in 1618 for King James I (Plate 219).

The present state shows the alterations made after the fire of London in 1666, which were necessitated by the damage resulting from the smoke and the heat (cf. *Samuel Pepys' Diary, 1668*). The large inscription tablet with the poem in praise of Henry VIII was added at that time, or during a later restoration, to replace the window; it is reproduced in the etching by Bernard Baron, published in 1736. The text was published by *R. H. Wornum* in *Life and Works of Hans Holbein, p. 352.*

In 1836, Passavant noted that the painting of the heads was excellent and that they could be restored to their original colour and perspective effect if properly treated (*Passavant, Tour of a German Artist in England, I, 270, London, 1836*). In 1895 Sir Charles Robinson in a letter to *The Times* wrote that in his opinion traces of Holbein's hand could be seen in all parts of the picture but an overpainting in the second half the of sixteenth century had changed the character of the work (*Chamberlain, II, 292*). Two copies with the window, one of which may be identical with the one ordered in 1618 by James I, are in the Royal College of Surgeons (Plate 219); A copy of the king in half-length with crown and sword belongs to the Duke of Bedford at Woburn Abbey.

INDEX TO PORTRAITS
AND
INDEX OF COLLECTIONS

INDEX TO PORTRAITS

(The numbers refer to the Catalogue)

INDEX OF COLLECTIONS

(The numbers refer to the Catalogue)